# GREENWICH'S MILITARY HERITAGE

David C. Ramzan

AMBERLEY

First published 2026

Amberley Publishing
The Hill, Stroud
Gloucestershire, GL5 4EP

www.amberley-books.com



Logo source material courtesy of Gerry van Tonder



ISBN 978 1 3981 2869 9 (print)
ISBN 978 1 3981 2870 5 (ebook)



British Library Cataloguing in Publication Data.
A catalogue record for this book is available from the British Library.

Typesetting by SJmagic DESIGN SERVICES, India.
Printed in Great Britain.

Appointed GPSR EU Representative: Easy Access System Europe Oü, 16879218
Address: Mustamäe tee 50, 10621, Tallinn, Estonia
Contact Details: gpsr.requests@easproject.com, +358 40 500 3575

# Contents

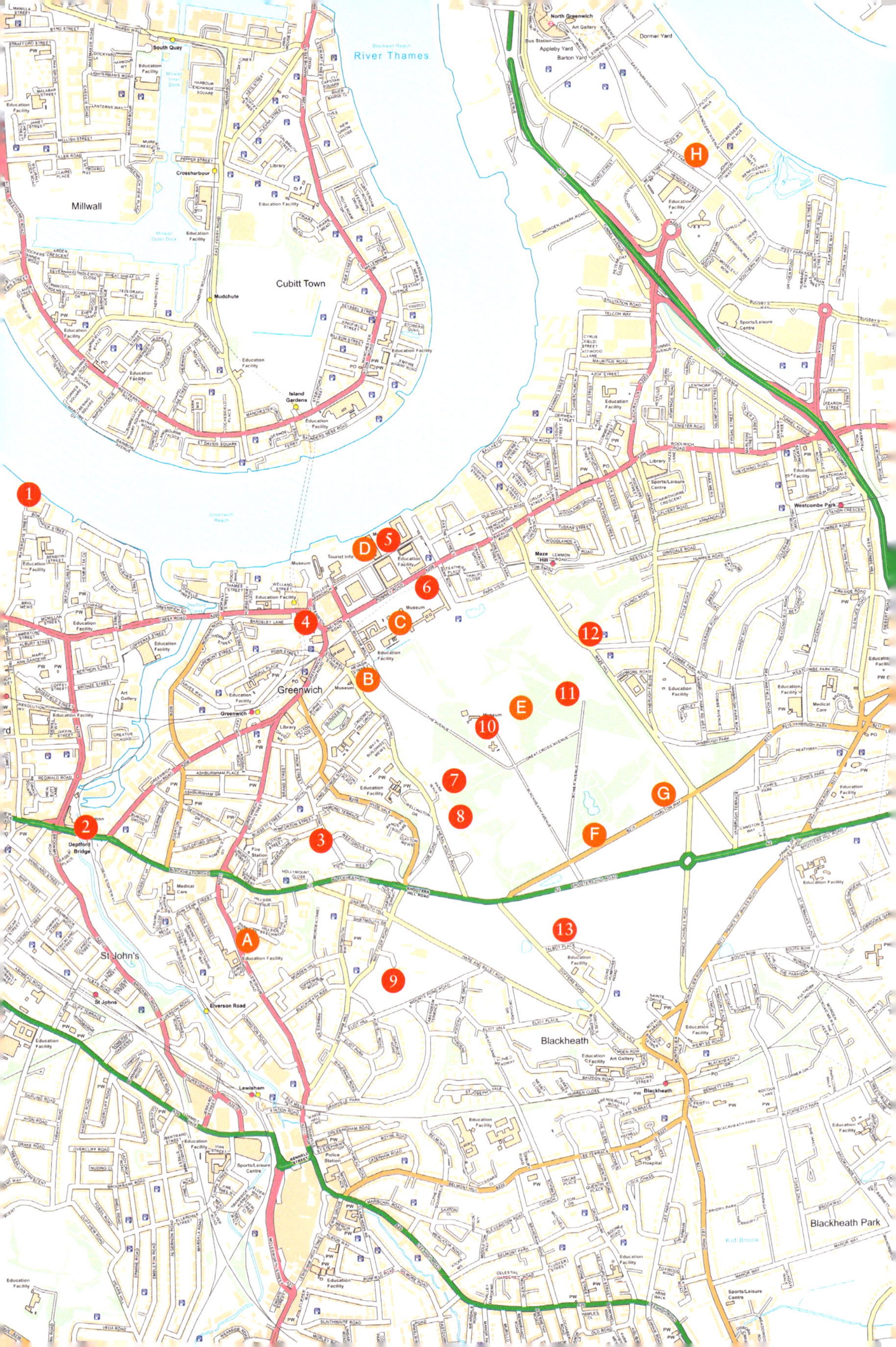

River Thames
Millwall
Cubitt Town
South Quay
Crossharbour
Mudchute
Island Gardens
North Greenwich
Greenwich
Maze Hill
Westcombe Park
Deptford Bridge
St John's
Elverson Road
Lewisham
Blackheath
Blackheath Park

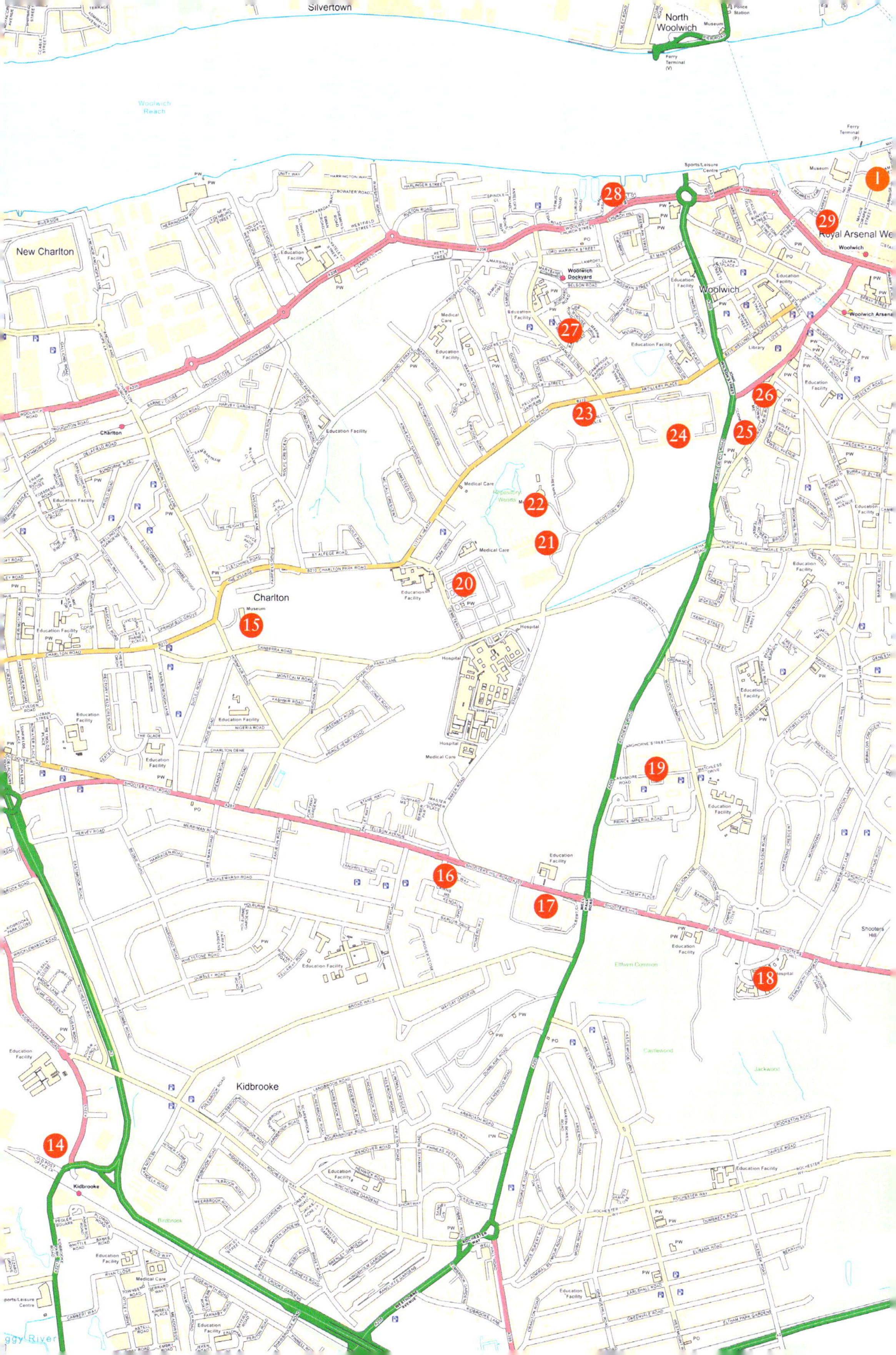

Silvertown
North Woolwich
Woolwich Reach
New Charlton
Charlton
Woolwich
Royal Arsenal West
Woolwich Dockyard
Woolwich Arsenal
Repository Woods
Eltham Common
Castlewood
Jackwood
Shooters Hill
Kidbrooke
Birdbrook
1
14
15
16
17
18
19
20
21
22
23
24
25
26
27
28
29

# Key

1. Deptford Royal Dockyard site
2. Battle of Deptford Bridge site
3. Deneholes site
4. St Alfege Church
5. Greenwich Royal Hospital/Old Royal Naval College
6. Royal Hospital School/National Maritime Museum
7. Saxon burial mounds
8. Macartney House
9. Holly Hedge House site
10. Old Royal Observatory
11. Romano-Celtic Temple site
12. Vanbrugh Castle
13. Battle of Blackheath site and Whitefield's Mount
14. RAF Kidbrooke site
15. Charlton House
16. Former Brook Hospital
17. Former Royal Herbert Hospital
18. Memorial Hospital
19. Former Royal Military Academy
20. Shrapnel Barracks site
21. Napier Barracks
22. Rotunda
23. Former Green Hill Barracks
24. Royal Artillery Barracks
25. St George's Church
26. Former Connaught Barracks
27. Red Barracks gates
28. Woolwich Royal Dockyard site
29. Woolwich Royal Arsenal site

## Memorials and Statues

A. Battle of Deptford Bridge memorial
B. King William IV
C. Devonport House memorials
D. Pepys Building medallion busts, Sir Walter Raleigh statue, New Zealand Wars memorial
E. General James Wolfe
F. Cornish Rebellion plaque
G. Blackheath war memorial
H. East Greenwich gasworks memorial
I. Woolwich Board of Ordnance memorial

# Introduction

As a youngster born and raised in Greenwich, I was surrounded by history: the Britons, Romans, Danes and Normans, the magnificent buildings of the Royal Naval College, the National Maritime Museum and Royal Observatory and to the west and east of the Meridian Line running through Greenwich, the former Royal Dockyards of Deptford and Woolwich.

My mother's family were Deptford residents, living close to the high street, where ship captains and members of the Royal Navy hierarchy once resided before the dockyard closed.

Woolwich, just a short bus ride away from my parents' home in Greenwich, was famous for its military establishments near the dockyard: the Royal Arsenal, Royal Military Academy, and various military barracks. Many of my ancestors had either been employed at these military establishments or had served in Britain's military forces, including those working in subsidiary industrial manufacturers situated throughout the borough and along the riverside.

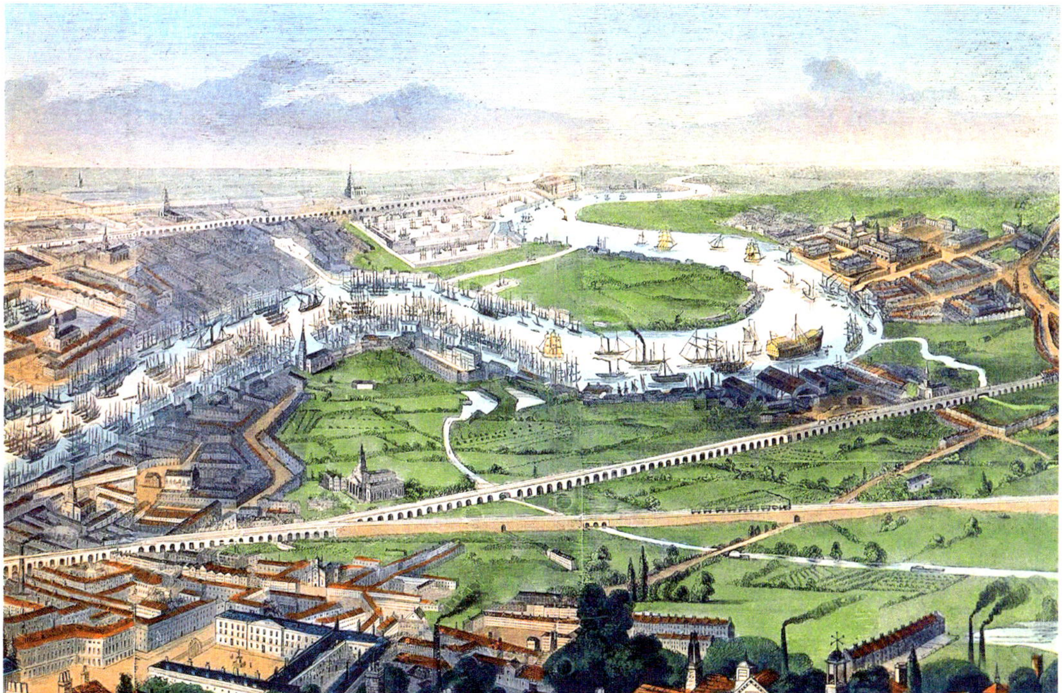

Deptford, Greenwich, and Woolwich *c.* 1800.

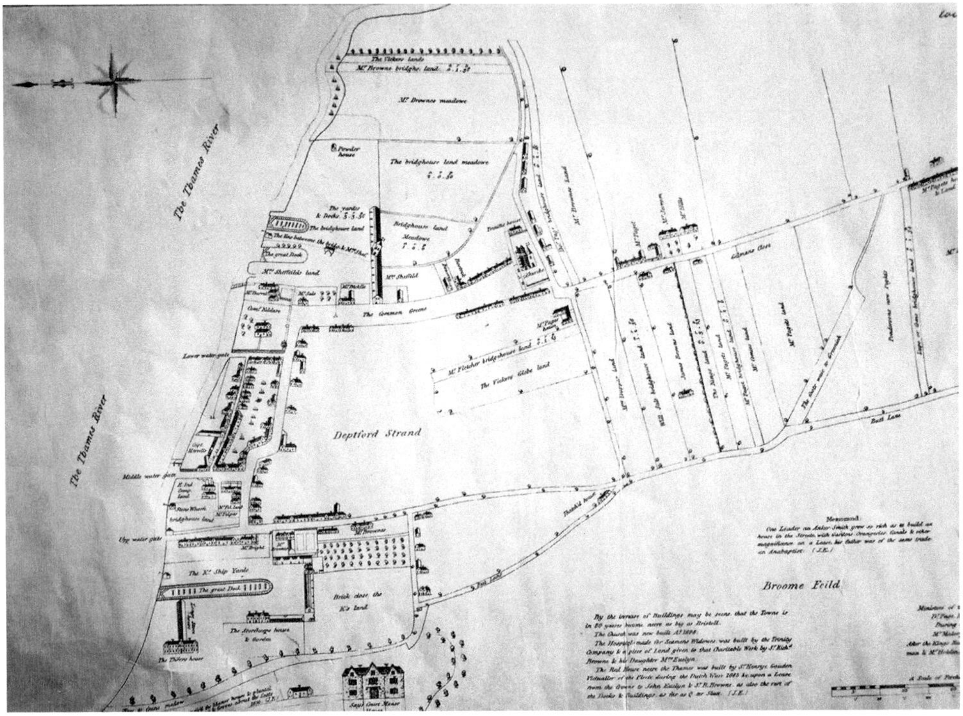


Deptford Royal Dockyard, late 1700s.

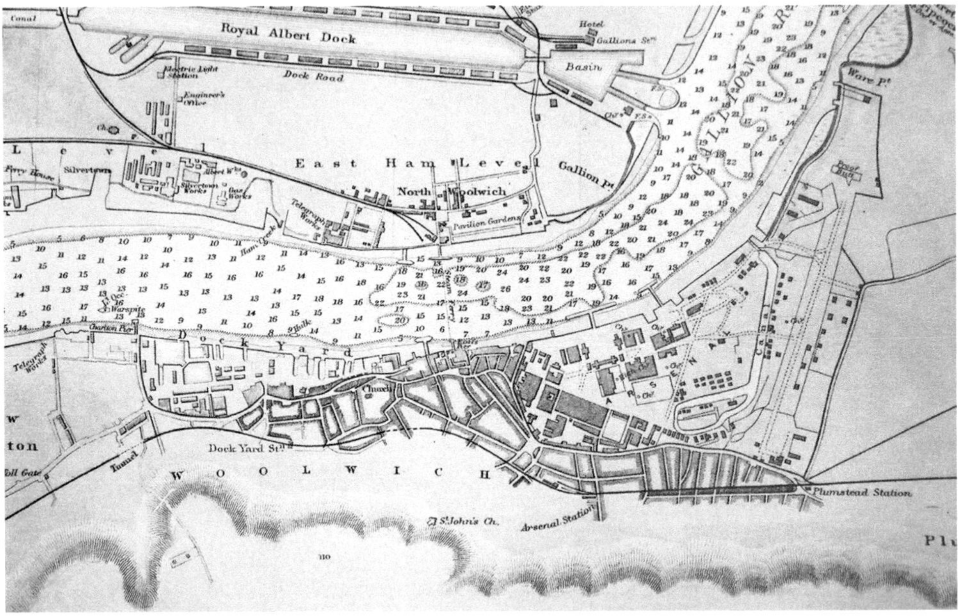


Woolwich Royal Dockyard and Royal Arsenal site, late 1800s.

To the south of my father's family residence was Greenwich Park, where my friends and I as youngsters would ride our bikes up and down the undulating hills close to many Saxon burial mounds and the remains of a Romano temple, both near ancient Watling Street.

At Blackheath, south of the park, my friends and I also often played in an area known by us as 'cowboy land', a large dip of gravel, sand and shrubs, the gravel originally dug to provide ballast for trade vessels moored on the Thames, the landscape about it rich in history, rebellion, battle and war, where king and barons fought lord and serfs.

Situated approximately 130 feet above the river, Blackheath had a commanding view towards London, an ideal location for the placement of searchlights, anti-aircraft guns, and barrage balloons during the Second World War.

Since those early times living in Greenwich, I now often visit Blackheath Tea Hut and, with a mug of tea in hand, gaze down towards the river and the capital far off in the distance, reminiscing over bygone times and reflecting on the rich heritage and historic places of my hometown.

In this publication I hope to reveal some of Greenwich's fascinating and unrivalled military history, along with the roles the Royal Navy, Royal Air Force and army played in the heritage of this riverside borough.

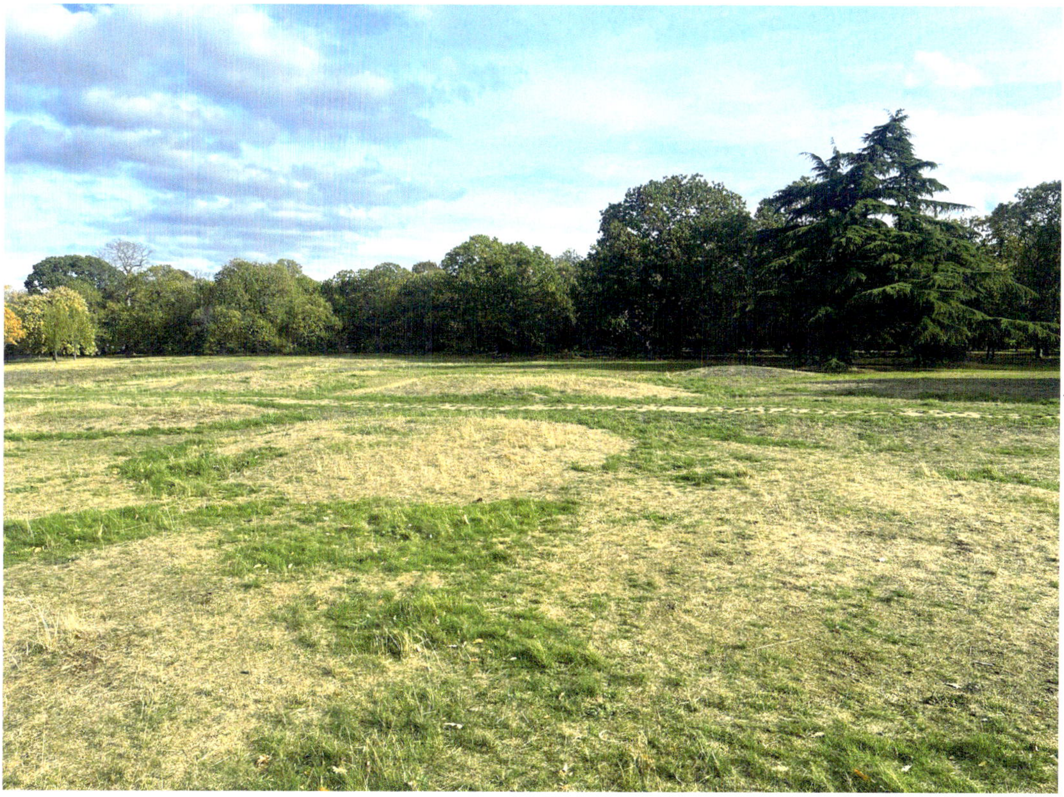

Saxon burial mounds.

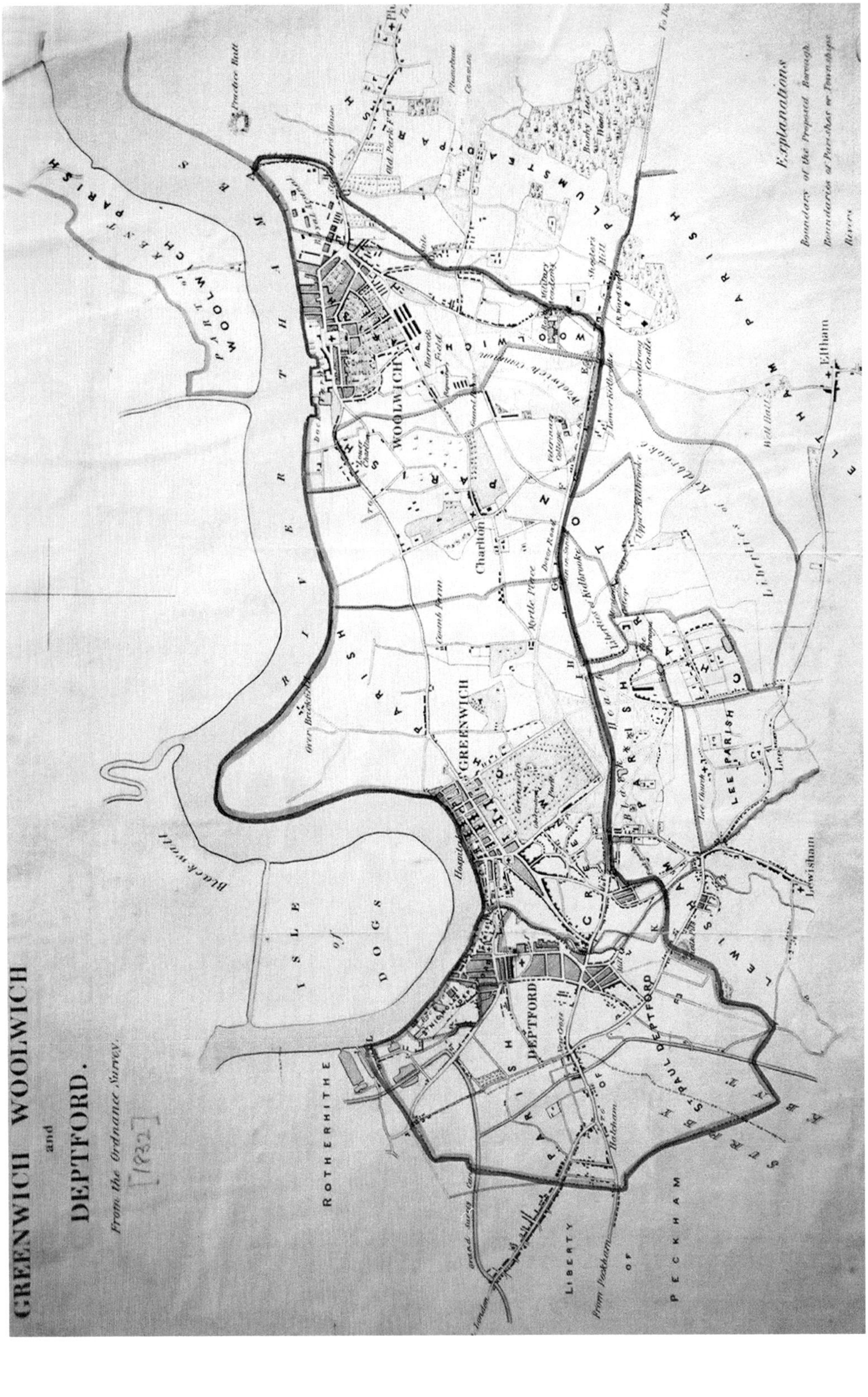


Borough of Greenwich boundary, *c.* 1832.

# 1. A Passage Through Time

Before the Roman occupation of Britain in 55 BC, archaeological evidence suggests Neolithic, Bronze Age and Iron Age activity within the landscape now recognised as the Royal Borough of Greenwich, the area's military history beginning after an abandoned Iron Age settlement at Woolwich was repurposed as an auxiliary fort by the Romans. A Romano-Celtic temple, dating to AD 100, was erected at the top of a hill, now within Greenwich Park, close to Watling Street, where Rome's military legions could stop to worship during their march towards Londinium. There is further evidence of Roman occupation within the grounds of the Old Royal Naval College and at Blackheath and Charlton.

After Rome's legions departed Britain at the beginning of the fourth century, Angles, Jutes and Saxons moved in from the east, gradually displacing remaining tribes of Britons. At a small inlet on the south side of the Thames, Anglo-Saxon settlers established a fishing village next to the river, named Gronewic in the Anglo-Saxon charter of 918, one of several Anglo-Saxon communities south of the Thames.

Greenwich had long associations with Anglo-Saxon royalty. Alfred the Great, great-grandson of King Ealhmund of Kent, inherited Greenwich from his father, Aethelwulf, the land passing to Alfred's daughter, Aelfthryth, on her marriage to Baldwin II, Count of Flanders. It is believed Aelfthryth later gifted her land – Grenevec (Greenwich), Uulwich (Woolwich) and Lieuesham (Lewisham) – to St Peter's Abbey Ghent.

Recorded in the Anglo-Saxon Chronicle of 964 as Grenewic (meaning green trading place or harbour), Greenwich had become a well-established Anglo-Saxon settlement where, on a plateau overlooking the Thames, in what is now Greenwich Park, Anglo-Saxons were laid to rest with their swords and shields in barrows previously used for Bronze Age burials.

By the early ninth century, marauding Scandinavian raiders, now known as Vikings, began sailing longships up the Thames towards London, one party mooring vessels off Greenwich, establishing an encampment on the hillside above the small settlement.

Greenwich remained a riverside fishing hamlet up until the Norman invasion, when the country was divided into manors ruled over by barons. Bishop Odo was gifted the manor of Greenwich by his half-brother, William I.

By the reign of Edward I, a royal lodging had been established at Greenwich, regularly visited for hunting trips by a succession of reigning monarchs. During the reign of Henry V, his brother, Humphrey, Duke of Gloucester, built the Palace of Placentia close to the river, enclosing the hunting park and erecting a fortified castle tower at its centre.

After Henry Tudor seized the crown at the Battle of Bosworth Field in 1485, the newly crowned king rebuilt the Palace of Placentia as a royal residence, ideally situated close to the king's ship repair yard at West Greenwich, now known as Deptford.

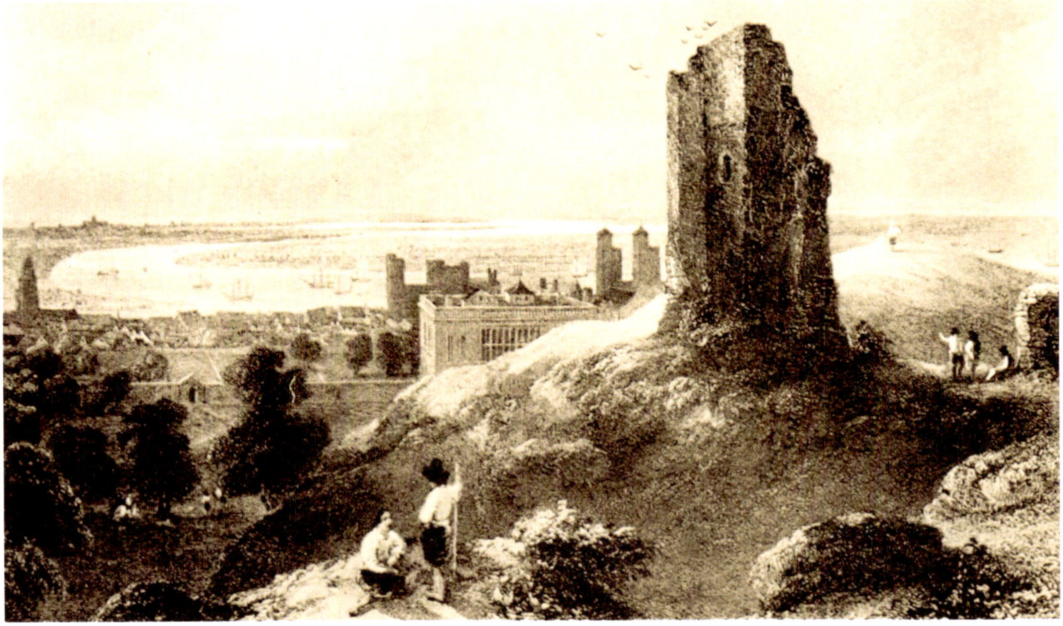

Greenwich Castle, mid-1600s.

Following Henry VII's death, his second son, Henry, was crowned king in 1509 and began a grand shipbuilding programme to further his father's shipbuilding plans. Henry VIII expanded the dockyard at Deptford and founded Woolwich Royal Dockyard, for the construction of the *Henry Grace á Dieu*, a warship named in memory of his father, the ship referred to as *Great Harry*.

To complement the Royal Dockyard at Woolwich, the grounds of a mid-sixteenth-century manor house known as the Warren were acquired by the Office of Ordnance, first to store guns, then expanding into the development and manufacture of gunpowder, and later the design and construction of large guns.

During the English Civil War, Greenwich Palace fell into disrepair, and following the Restoration of Charles II, a magnificent Palladian-style series of buildings was planned to replace the old palace buildings. Initially intended as a new palace for Charles II, when William and Mary came to the throne in 1689 the project was completed under the queen's direction as a hospital for injured and retired naval tars. On the opposite side of the main Greenwich thoroughfare, two wings were added to the seventeenth-century Queen's House for the education of boy sailors in navigation, science, and modern naval warfare.

From Deptford through Greenwich onto Woolwich, by the early 1800s, military presence in the borough was without equal.

The small harbour town of Woolwich had grown rapidly, through the expansion of the Arsenal site and Royal Dockyard, from the riverside and on towards Shooters Hill, and by the mid-1900s, Woolwich came under the control of the borough of Greenwich.

Woolwich town was made up of an assortment of various shops and dwellings, a majority built to serve military forces. The military establishments consisted of various regimental

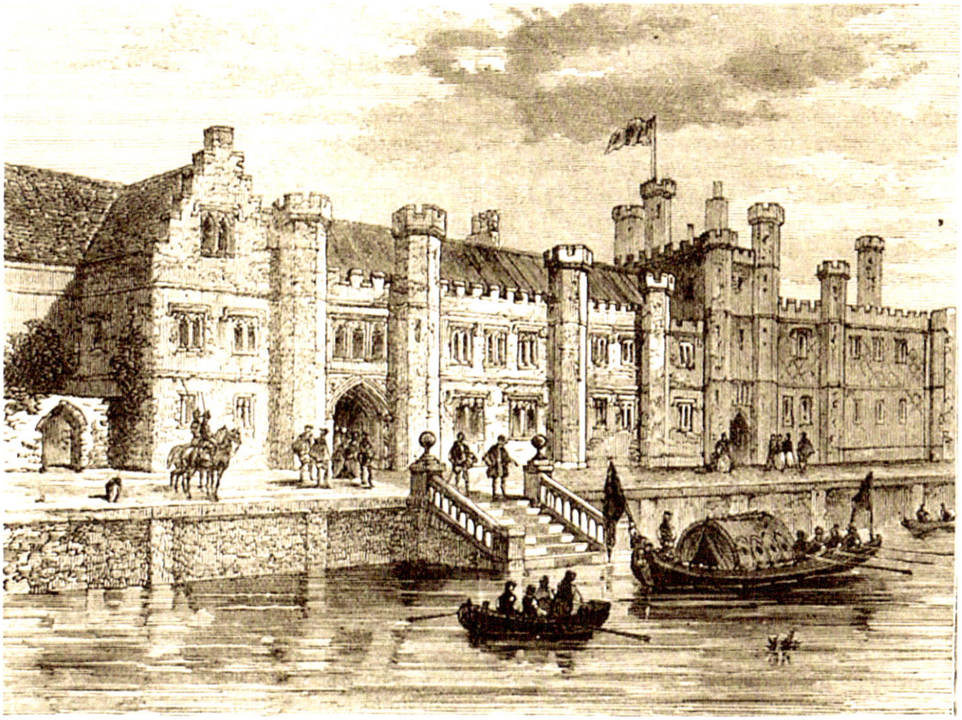

Rebuilt Palace of Placentia, late 1400s.

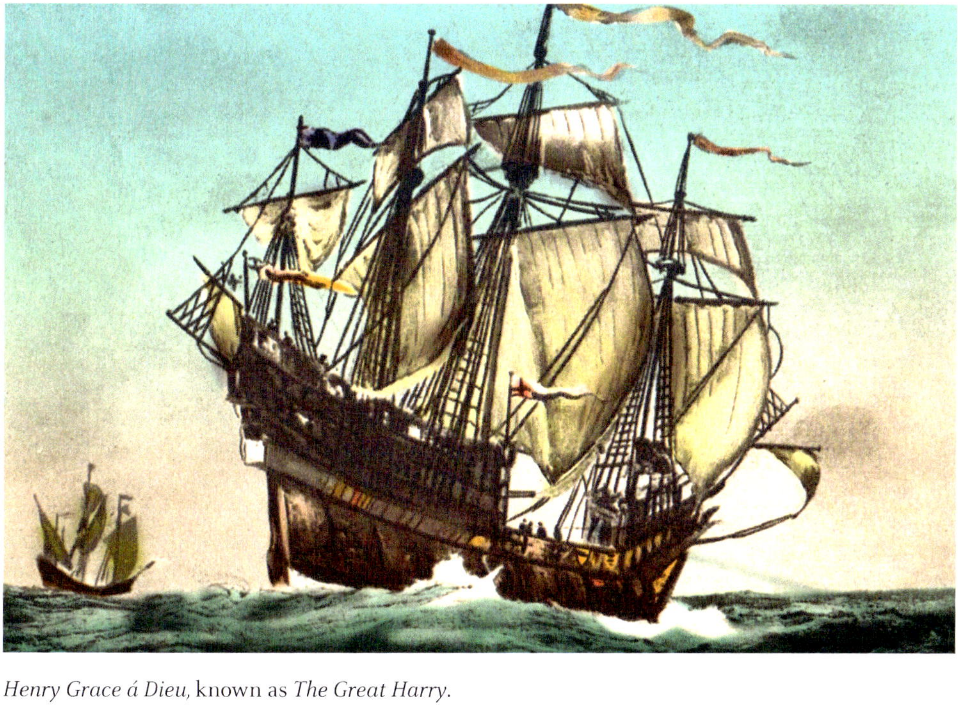

*Henry Grace á Dieu*, known as *The Great Harry*.

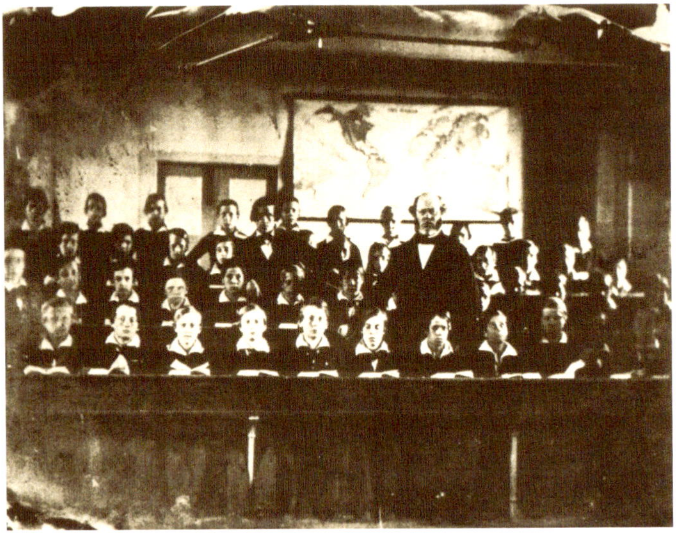

The Greenwich Hospital School class, mid-1800s.

barracks, army hospitals and training facilities, ordinance depots, and places of worship, along with prison hulks moored off Woolwich, the prisoners engaged in hard labour.

Greenwich had gradually encroached east into Woolwich, west into Deptford and south towards Blackheath, Lewisham and Eltham, constituted as a metropolitan borough in 1889, a World Heritage Site in 1997, and a Royal Borough in 2012. Through the centuries, Greenwich's military heritage has significantly influenced and shaped the lives of its residents and those who worked and served in the armed forces.

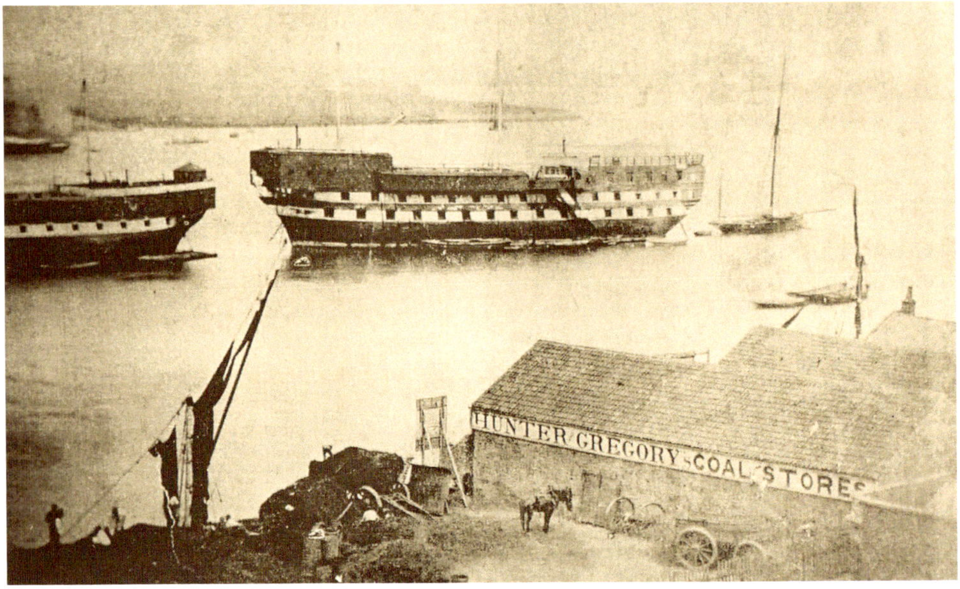


Convict hulk *Unite* moored off Woolwich, late 1800s.

# 2. Local Conflicts

Although there is evidence the Romans settled at many places across the Greenwich landscape, they likely co-existed alongside local tribal settlements, the kingdom of Kent, which at that time included Greenwich, ruled over by the Canti. To date, there has been no indication of hostilities between Britons and Romans.

The auxiliary fort at Woolwich was most likely established to protect the port and Roman trading activities from hostile attacks by raiders on the Thames.

The earliest recorded conflict occurred after the Romans departed Britain and the Anglo-Saxons settled along the south bank of the river. After a period of calm and stability under Anglo-Saxon rule, Scandinavians began making assaults along the coast of Britain in the late eighth century, pillaging and looting monasteries and churches rich in gold and silver artefacts. When a fleet of longships sailed up the Thames towards Anglo-Saxon-held London at the beginning of the eleventh century, several moored off Greenwich, the Danes establishing a camp above the river on a hillside close to Blackheath.

The Danes made raids inland southwards, laying siege to Canterbury, sacking the city, and taking Anglo-Saxon Archbishop Alfege hostage. After returning to their Greenwich camp, Alfege was ransomed for money. Knowing his people would be left impoverished if they paid the 3,000 gold marks demanded, Alfege refused to be ransomed. Held captive for six months, during a feast coinciding with Easter, frustrated and in a state of drunkenness, the Danes pelted Alfege with animal bones from their meal, then beat him with axe shafts.

One Dane, believed to be a Christian convert, out of compassion, struck Alfege on the head with the back of an axe, killing the archbishop instantly. Alfege's death was condemned throughout Christendom, nowhere more so than St Peter's Abbey at Ghent, titleholders to the manor of Greenwich.

Canonised in 1078, a place of worship was built on the spot where Alfege died, dedicated to the martyred archbishop, the small, humble structure later replaced by a magnificent eighteenth-century church designed by Nicholas Hawksmoor.

To the south of where the Danes had once camped, a contingent of Kent rebels marching from Canterbury in 1381, led by Kent-born Wat Tyler, met with government representatives at Blackheath to protest against high taxation and demand financial and social reform. Unsuccessful, Wat Tyler and the rebels marched on London. The rebels, joined by local townsfolk, set fire to the temple and the law books, killing those who opposed them, including Lord Chancellor Simon Sudbury and Lord High Treasurer Robert Hales. After the rebels had gained access to the Tower of London, Sudbury and Hales were beheaded on Tower Hill.

To appease the rebels, fourteen-year-old King Richard II agreed to many demands, including the abolition of serfdom. However, when Tyler met with the king at Smithfield, violence broke out over terms of settlement and Tyler was attacked by the king's men and severely wounded.

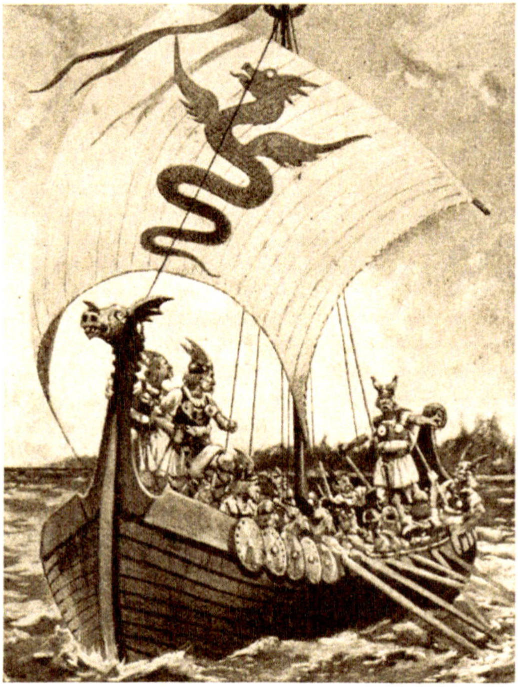

*Left*: Viking raider longship, late eighth century.

*Below left*: St Alphege Church, West Greenwich, erected 1712–14.

*Below right*: Wat Tyler confronts mother of Richard II during rebel's march on London in 1381.

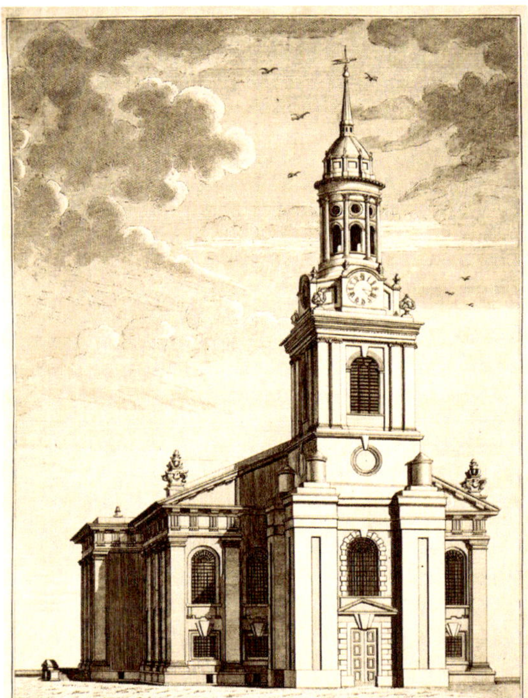


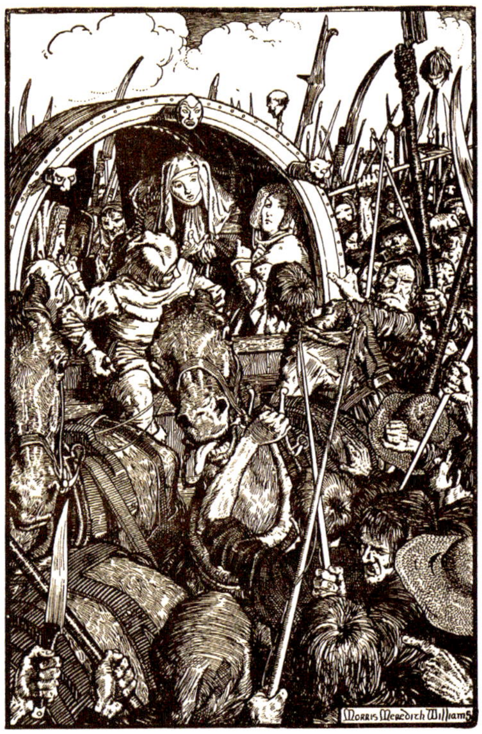

Making his escape on horseback, Tyler was tracked down and dragged back to Smithfield, and unceremoniously beheaded. The rebels were driven from the city, many killed making their way back to Blackheath, the survivors dispersing into the Kent countryside.

Just under 100 years later, Sussex-born Jack Cade led a contingent of men to Blackheath after defeating a force of King Henry VI's men-at-arms at Sevenoaks, in a rebellion against the corrupt governance of the king. Known as the Peasants' Insurrection of 1450, Cade assembled reinforcements from where support was at its strongest, including men from north Kent, the encampment on Blackheath consisting of around 5,000 men. Cade set up headquarters in a cavern below the heath. After a month mustering forces, Cade marched on London and the rebels took control of the city.

When disorder broke out amongst the rebels, London's citizens, although sympathetic to the rebel cause, mustered on the capital's streets, forcing the rebels back across London Bridge, the rebellion falling into disarray.

Even though Cade and his rebels were pardoned by the king, on his return to Sussex Cade was ambushed and killed by the future Sheriff of Kent. After Cade's death, Blackheath Cavern, where Cade held counsel, became a shrine to his memory. The caverns were believed to have originated as Deneholes, chalk mines.

Southern Greenwich became the battleground of the last campaign fought by Celtic warriors in London, known as the Battle of Blackheath, which took place in June 1497.

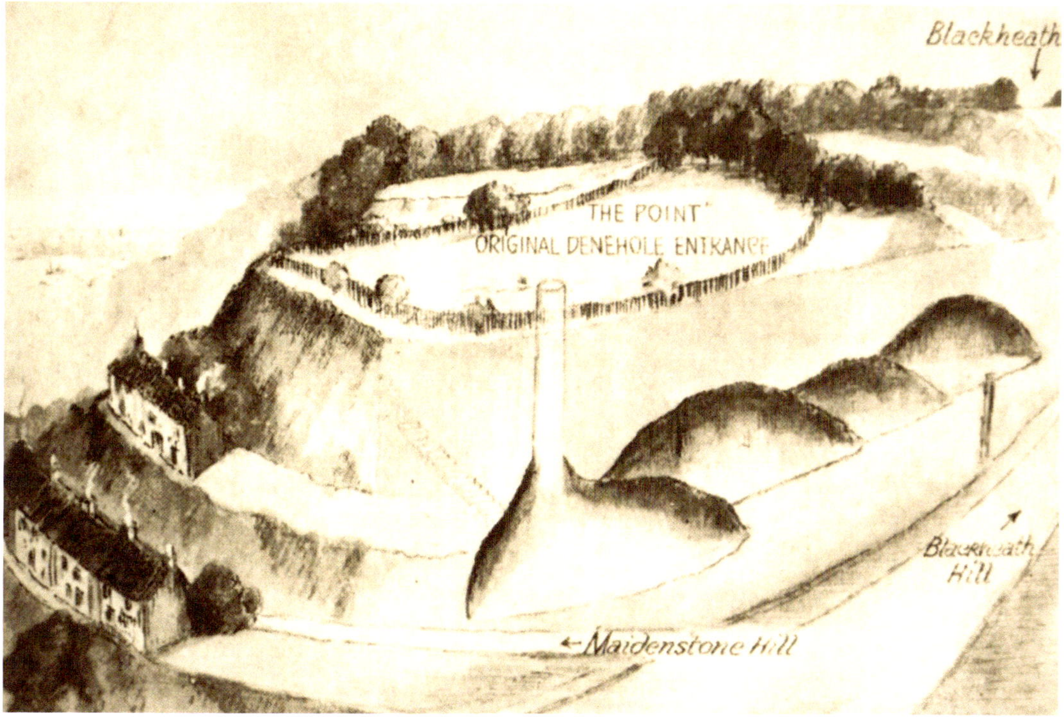


Blackheath caves (Deneholes), mid-1800s.

The rebels, numbering around 15,000, led by Baron James Tuchet, Thomas Flamank, and Michael An Gof, faced a force of Henry VII's soldiers, numbering at least 25,000, commanded by the king and seasoned campaigner Lord Daubeney. The uprising was the result of heavy taxes imposed on the lower classes to fund the king's war against the Scots, with Cornwall particularly hard hit. Many rebels were recruited from the western counties, Cornish archers joining the cause, and on their march towards London the rebels gathered more support before encamping on Blackheath.

On the day of the battle, the king and Lord Daubeney, waiting below Blackheath near Deptford Strand with three battalions of men, advance upon the rebels across Deptford Bridge, defended by rebel Cornish archers. Although a volley of arrows loosed by the archers caused severe casualties to a battalion of spearmen commanded by Sir Humphrey Stanley, Daubney led an attack against the rebels' main position on Blackheath.

During a skirmish, Daubeney was captured; however, when released without harm, he rallied his troops in a counterattack, the rebels encircled by a detachment of soldiers led by the Earl of Oxford, John de Vere. It was estimated 2,000 rebels were slain during the battle, many from the ranks of Cornish archers, with a further 1,500 men taken prisoner, the remainder taking flight. Following the battle, Henry VII rode across Blackheath's battlefield, knighting those of his men he considered had fought most bravely.

The rebel leaders, Tuchet, Flamank, and An Gof, were captured and executed, their heads impaled on spikes displayed on London Bridge. Allegedly, countless bodies of the slain West Country warriors were buried at a place known today as Whitfield's Mound, subsequently used over the following years as a rallying point for protests and preaching.

During the reign of the Tudors, it was common for battles and skirmishes to be staged for the entertainment of the royal court at Greenwich. In 1516, during Henry VIII's May

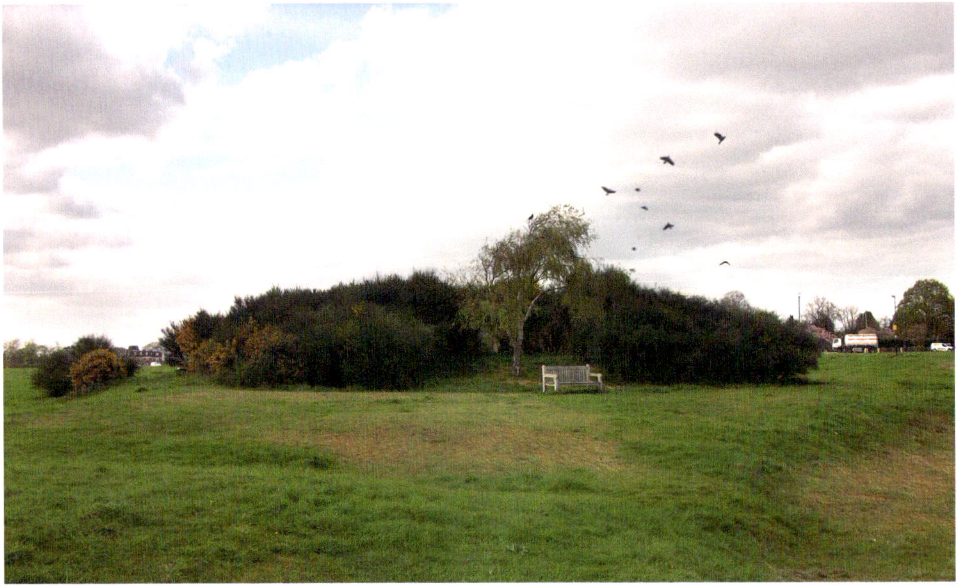

Whitefield's Mount, Blackheath.

Day ride out from Greenwich Palace, the king and his first queen, Catherine, accompanied by members of the royal court, encountered a party of outlaws in the forest near Shooters Hill. Dressed in green, the tall yeomen, carrying bows and arrows, their number estimated to be around 200, were led by one declaring to be none other than Robin Hood. The outlaw asked his highness if he desired to see his men shoot their arrows, and when the king agreed they shot simultaneously, causing a great whistling noise in the air, much to the amusement of the king and his entourage.

The archers were not outlaws but members of Henry's own guard, putting on a show to entertain the king. After the display, the royal entourage was invited to dine on venison and wine with Robin Hood and his Merry Men.

The king's father, Henry VII, had previously held archery competitions at Greenwich Park during the annual Grand May Day Games and to encourage the continued use of the bow. Henry VIII ordered his Master of Ordnance to form the 'Fraternitye or Guylde of Saint George' of 'longbows, crossbows and handgonnes', a military company second oldest in the world to the Vatican's Pontifical Swiss Guard.

During the reign of Elizabeth I, the fraternity was renamed the Honourable Artillery Company, and for over 200 years archery continued to be practised even when the musket replaced the longbow as a handheld weapon of war. After Elizabeth's coronation in July 1559, an elaborate programme of entertainment at Greenwich Palace included a staged military battle and tilt competition, with Sir Henry Lee, representing the queen, becoming her first champion.

During the following three centuries, there were no further recorded localised military conflicts, apart from staged reenactments and pageants celebrating military anniversaries and commemorations.

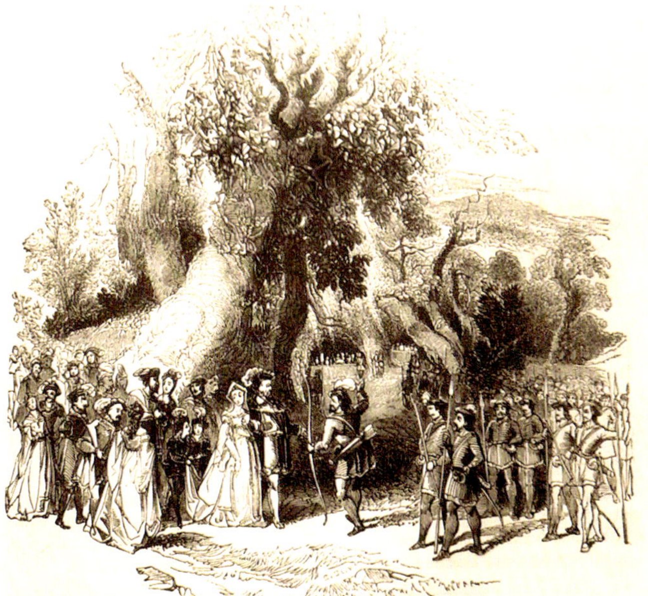

*Henry VIII. Maying at Shooters' Hill.*

Henry VIII meets Robin Hood, May 1515.

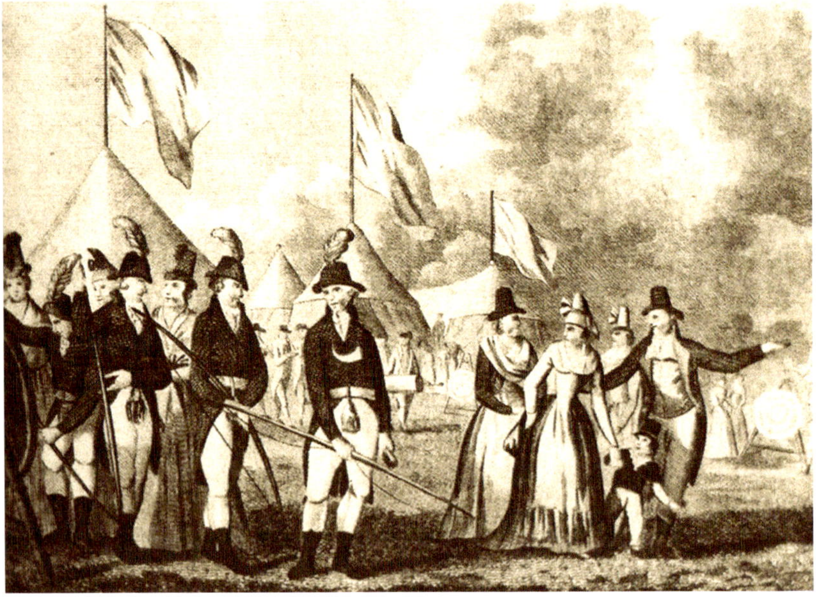

Blackheath Archers, *c.* 1850.

On the afternoon of 15 February 1894, what is considered the first act of international terrorism within British shores occurred in Greenwich Park.

French national Martial Bourdin, carrying a small package containing a bomb, entered the park when, on nearing the Royal Observatory, the bomb exploded in his hand. Suffering from severe injuries, including the loss of a hand, Bourdin was taken on a stretcher to the Seaman's Hospital close by, where he later died. Investigations by the police discovered the Frenchman was a member of the Club Autonomie situated in London, the members consisting of foreign anarchists.

Just under 100 years after this first terrorist bomb explosion, the Provisional Irish Republican Army targeted the King's Arms public house at Woolwich in 1974. The pub, situated on the corner of Frances Street and Hill Reach, had been a favoured drinking place over many years of squaddies stationed at the army barracks opposite.

The explosion from a gelignite bomb thrown through the pub window killed two people, Gunner Richard Dunne of the Royal Artillery and salesclerk Alan Horsley, the bomb also injured thirty-eight others, including pub landlady Margaret Nash.

In January 1979, the Provisional IRA exploded two bombs at the East Greenwich Gas Works, damaging both huge gasholders, the largest later demolished. In the IRA's continuation of its overseas offensive, another bomb exploded at the Royal Artillery Barracks in December 1983, while a Christmas party was taking place in the Sergeant's Mess. Although on this occasion there were no fatalities, the explosion injured five people.

A further act of terrorism occurred on the afternoon of 22 May 2013, when off-duty Fusilier, drummer Lee Rigby of the Royal Regiment of Fusiliers, while walking along Wellington Street near the Royal Artillery Barracks, was attacked and killed by Islamic extremists. Both attackers were arrested at the scene and after tried and found guilty of murder, were sentenced to life imprisonment.

# 3. Foreign Conflicts

With all three branches of Britain's military services once based in the Borough of Greenwich, the history of overseas conflicts goes back to an initial period of the riverside town's existence.

Both Henry VII and, later, his son Henry VIII planned and executed foreign policy strategies from the royal court at Greenwich Palace. Many ships engaged in defending home waters from overseas threats or employed in fighting sea battles, along with transporting troops to distant shores, were built and maintained at the nearby dockyards of Deptford and Woolwich.

Henry VII's main aim during his reign, however, was to avoid waging war overseas. The French, allied to Scotland, were a much wealthier nation than the kingdom Henry ruled, and with the king's weak claim to the English throne he did not wish to engage in conflicts that may lose him the crown. Italy and Spain were powerful rival trading countries, and with diplomacy considered the most prudent way forward, Henry established a compact and well-equipped fleet of ships and men to expand trade overseas. Nevertheless, in 1492, Henry was forced into a conflict he did not want, in protection of semi-independent duchy of Brittany, an ally of England, after occupation by French forces.

With a compliment of 26,000 men, Henry laid siege to Boulogne, and with a threat of asserting his claim to the French crown, a right dating back to the Hundred Years' War, King Charles of France signed a treaty where Brittany would remain under French rule and in return Henry received a pension of £5,000 a year, including assurances France would not support Perkin Warbeck, pretender to the English throne.

After Henry VII's death, the crown passed to eldest surviving son, Henry, as the first in line to the throne, Arthur, Prince of Wales, had died seven years before. Henry VIII, however, unlike his father, made a conscious effort to engage in various military conflicts, both home and overseas, to increase England's international standing and expand his influence by forging alliances with European royalty.

Henry went to war against the Scots, the Gaelic lords of Ireland, the French, and his own allies in the Low Countries. After being crowned king in 1509, Henry proceeded to make Greenwich Palace, where he was born, his main place of residence between 1512 and 1532, from where many plans were formulated to enhance England's power, prestige, and territorial expansion in Europe.

These conflicts resulted in the development of a powerful and modernised naval force and advancements in military technology. With many warships built at both Deptford and Woolwich, increasing the king's fleet, and the advancement of artillery and firearm production, England became one of the most powerful countries in the then known world.

However, Henry's military expansion came at great cost, plunging the English crown into huge debt. A year after taking up residence at Greenwich, Henry's first major campaign, the Battle of the Spurs, took place during August 1513, part of the Holy League during the ongoing Italian wars. Under the command of Henry and Maximilian I, self-proclaimed King of the Romans, their forces routed a body of French cavalry while besieging the town of Thérouanne in Artois. After the town fell, Henry besieged and took Tournai, Belgium, which came under English rule until 1519.

Henry, in league with Holy Roman Emperor Charles V, went to war in 1521 against Francis I of France and the Republic of Venice. The conflict arose when a French expedition attempted to retake Navarre, while the main French army invaded the Low Countries. An alliance was formed between Henry, the pope, and the Holy Roman Emperor when hostilities broke out on the Italian Peninsula. In 1522, at the Battle of Bicocca, near Milan, the forces of the alliance defeated the French and drove them out of Lombardy, northern Italy.

At Greenwich Palace, Henry founded a royal armoury in 1511, which produced a distinctively English style of plate armour known as Almain, originally created in Germany – the armour crafted by imported master armourers hired by the king.

Although armour made at Greenwich would have seen military use, it was mainly produced for the nobility to wear and compete in tournaments and jousting.

The armoury would go forward to make armour for Henry's second daughter, Elizabeth, who ascended to the throne in 1559. Elizabeth is said to have been wearing a plumed

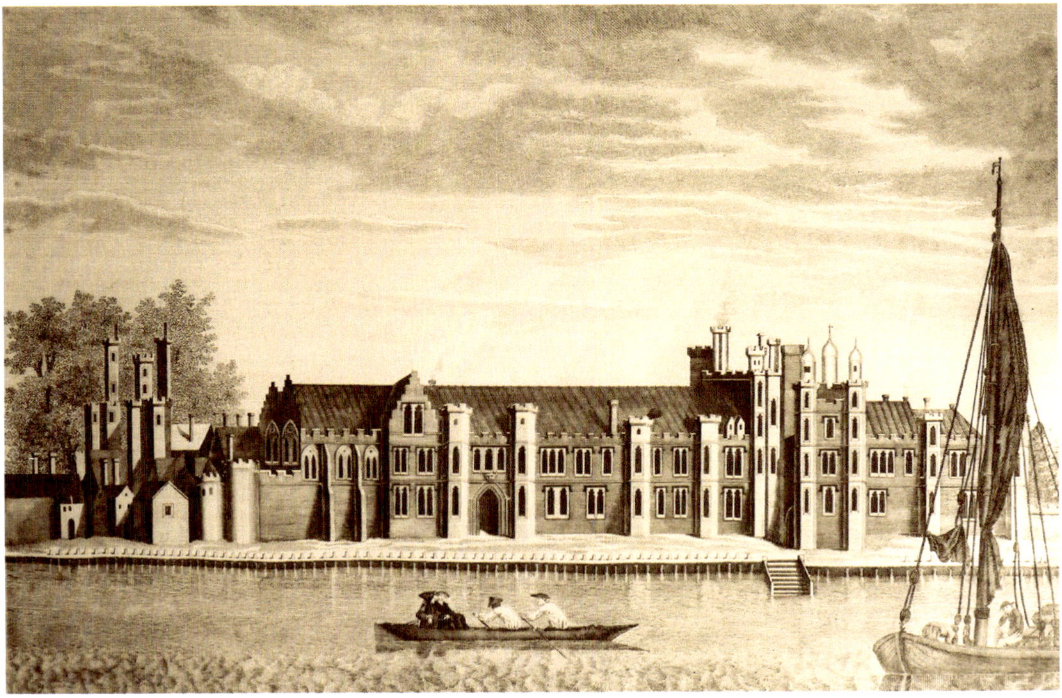

Greenwich Palace before the English Civil War.

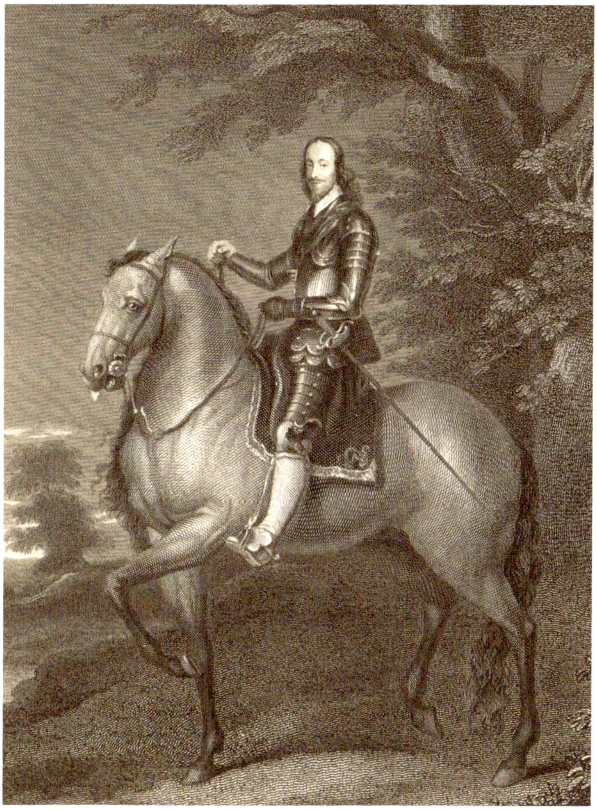

Greenwich armour made for Charles I, *c.* 1635. (Courtesy of the Wellcome Collection)

helmet and steel cuirass, armour worn over a white gown consisting of a breast plate and back plate fastened together, as she rode upon a white horse to address troops at Tilbury in readiness for an expected Spanish invasion.

Like her father, Elizabeth spent the early part of her reign at Greenwich Palace, meeting her councillors and military commanders and drawing up plans to repulse the ongoing threat from Spain, known as the Anglo-Spanish War. The intermittent conflict which raged from 1585 to 1604 was fuelled by religious differences between Protestant England and Catholic Spain, the principal military action during Elizabeth's reign the defeat of the Spanish Armada in 1588.

Those fighting men of war which took part in the routing of the Armada comprised of Deptford-built *Revenge*, commanded by Sir Francis Drake, the *Ark Royal, Ayde, Foresight, Rainbow*, and *Triumph*. One Woolwich-built ship, the *Vanguard*, played a key role in the action by engaging two larger, heavily armed galleons.

During the remainder of Elizabeth's reign, England participated in various conflicts overseas, as well as internally with the Scots and Irish, manoeuvring between alliances with France and Spain to balance power in Europe. However, Elizabeth's support of privateers, such as Drake, Hawkins, Raleigh, and Frobisher, engaging in attacks on Spanish shipping and colonial interests across the globe, continued to contribute to Anglo-Spanish rivalry up until the death of the queen in 1603.

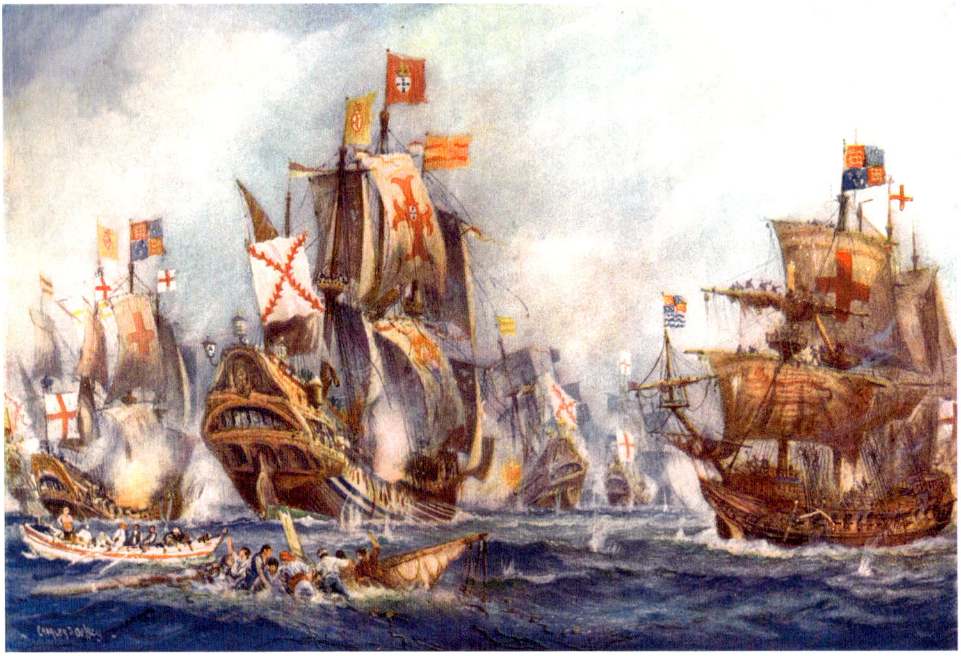

Defeat of the Spanish Armada, *c.* 1588.

As a memorial to Drake and his privateering exploits, the *Golden Hind* was moored at Deptford Creek as a museum until broken up in the mid-1600s.

After James VI of Scotland succeeded Elizabeth, the last Tudor monarch dying without an heir, the crowns of both Scotland and England were unified. Soon after succession, James moved his court to Greenwich Palace to be close to both shipbuilding yards of Deptford and Woolwich; however, the king would prioritise peace over war. Vessels built at the dockyards were more commonly a collection of royal and private trading ships, which, if required, could be called upon in time of war. Although James inherited a form of naval structure from his cousin Elizabeth, a potential for a strong fleet of naval ships was never realised, specifically as James would end the long war with Spain and avoid involvement in the Thirty Years' War, which ravaged much of central Europe, decisions which eased the country's financial spending.

This all changed after Charles I became king in 1625, when plans were made to attack Spanish colonies in the New World and capture ships laden with treasure. However, very few ships built at Deptford or Woolwich were employed in naval warfare during the king's reign; the vessels dispatched for exploration and colonisation consisted mostly of privately owned vessels commanded by military leaders rather than professional sailors.

George Villiers, the Duke of Buckingham, after being appointed Lord High Admiral by Charles I, was tasked with conducting naval expeditions overseas, several of the expeditionary fleet ships consisting of vessels built and fitted out at Deptford. Ultimately, these expeditions were failures, and the amount spent by the king in support of Villiers infuriated Members of Parliament. Charles provoked further unrest when attempting to raise taxes to aid naval defence without Parliamentary consent, one of several unpopular actions by the king which eventually led the country to internal conflict.

With the line of royalty holding court at Greenwich ending after the reign of Mary and William, and with the power to preside over military engagements overseas shifting from the monarchy to Parliament, the riverside town of Greenwich, encompassing Woolwich and Deptford, would soon become central to British military expeditions across the globe.

Charles II had previously reformed the navy as a national institution under the title the Royal Navy, and the expansion of both Royal Dockyards brought forth the opportunity for building various-sized and innovatively designed vessels, in a programme of shipbuilding to establish and defend the country's ever-expanding empire. These vessels included decoy ships, built to resemble merchantmen, equipped with guns hidden behind false bulkheads.

Throughout the eighteenth and nineteenth centuries, the Royal Navy was the largest maritime force in the world. Several hundred ships sailed out of the dockyards of Deptford and Woolwich patrolling the seaways to protect British merchant shipping from attack by corsairs, pirates and privateers. They also engaged in a series of seaborne offensives during times of war.

British naval supremacy was at its height during conflicts against the Spanish, Dutch, French, and colonies of the Americas during the War of Independence. Britain's most famous victory occurred against the combined French and Spanish fleets at the Battle of Trafalgar in October 1805.

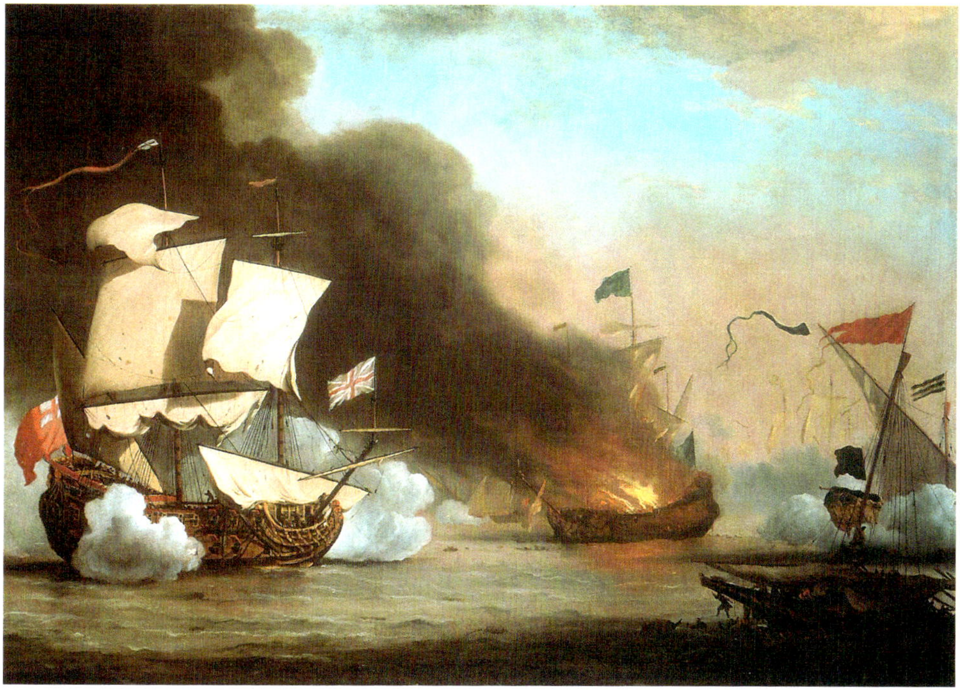

Woolwich-built fourth-rate British decoy ship *Kingfisher*, engaging Barbary pirates, *c.* 1680. (Courtesy of Dover Publications)

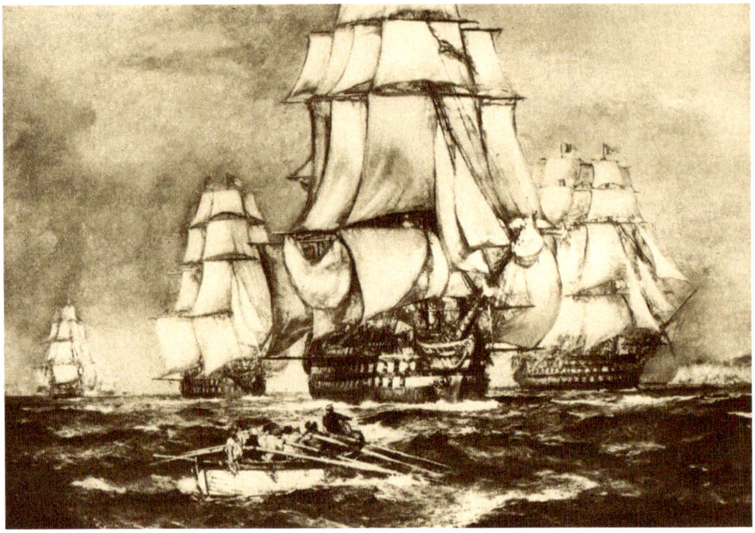

*Hearts of Oak* at the Battle of Trafalgar, October 1805.

Deptford-built ships that fought at Trafalgar included ninety-eight-gun second-rate ship of the line HMS *Neptune*, firing several broadsides into a succession of enemy ships; seventy-four-gun second-rate HMS *Colossus*, capturing the Spanish ship *Bahama*; seventy-four-gun third-rate HMS *Mars*, taking heavy fire from five different French and Spanish ships; and another seventy-four-gun third-rate ship of the line HMS *Orion*, forcing the surrender of the French ship *Intrépide*. The Woolwich-built HMS *Prince* engaged the Spanish flagship *Principe de Asturias* during the battle, as well as the French ship *Achille*, which caught fire and blew up. Another ship built at Woolwich, seventy-four-gun third-rate ship of the line HMS *Minotaur*, came to the aid of under fire HMS *Victory*, flagship of Admiral Nelson, her captain placing *Minotaur* between the damaged *Victory*

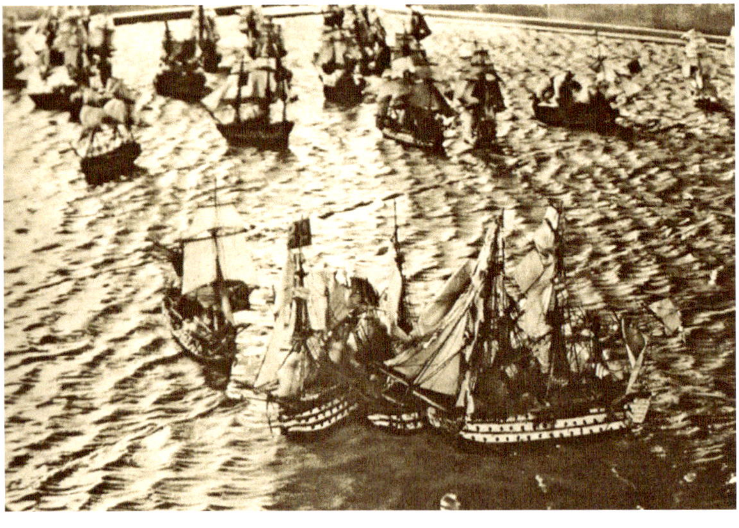

*Victory* under attack at the Battle of Trafalgar. This was made for an 1840 exhibition and was once displayed at the National Maritime Museum.

and an attacking French vessel. *Minotaur*'s captain, Charles Mansfield, was awarded a gold medal and sword for gallantry, both of which are held in the National Maritime Museum, Greenwich.

By the mid-1800s, the Thames riverbed, although continually dredged, suffered from heavy silting, and it became impractical to build large ships at Deptford and Woolwich dockyards, both eventually closed for shipbuilding, although the sites were used for storage and some maritime manufacturing and civil ship and boat building.

In support of British military actions in far-off lands, the Arsenal had supplied munitions, canons, guns, and supplies for both army and naval forces since the late seventeenth century. British Army units were stationed at the Arsenal working alongside civilians, and as the site expanded, officers and troops were stationed at barracks outside the Arsenal site, the barracks evolved and grew as British interests expanded across the globe. The barracks at Woolwich would include the Royal Artillery Barracks, Green Hill

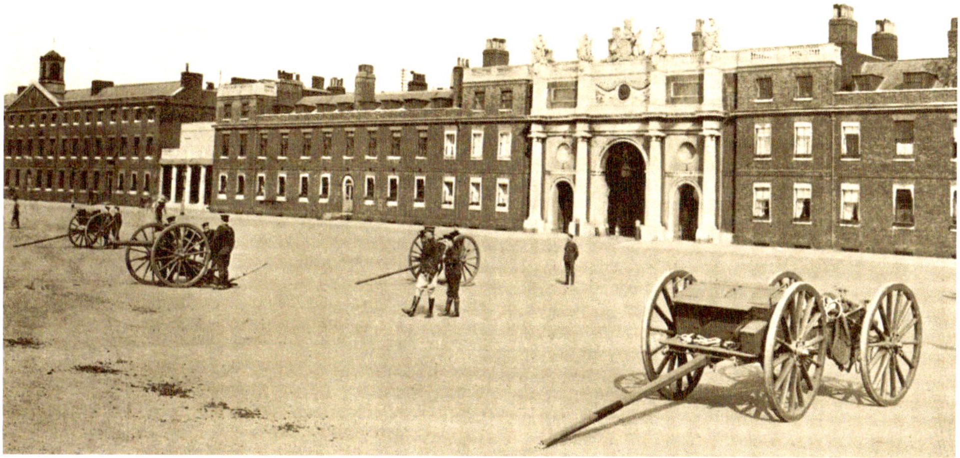

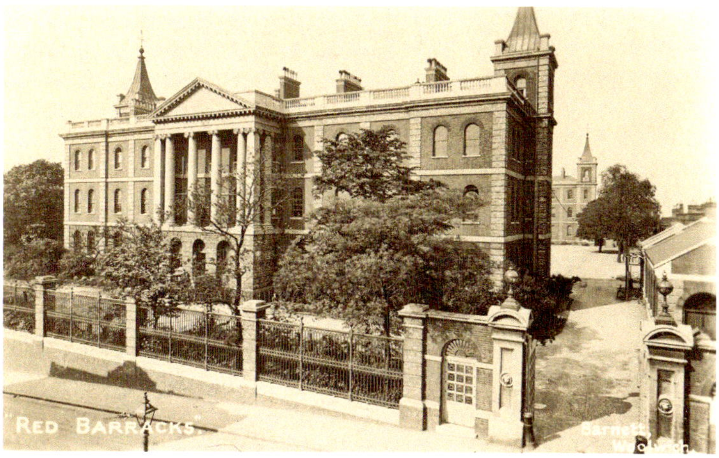


*Above*: Royal Artillery Barracks, Woolwich Common, *c*. 1800.

*Right*: Red Barracks off Frances Street, *c*. 1800.

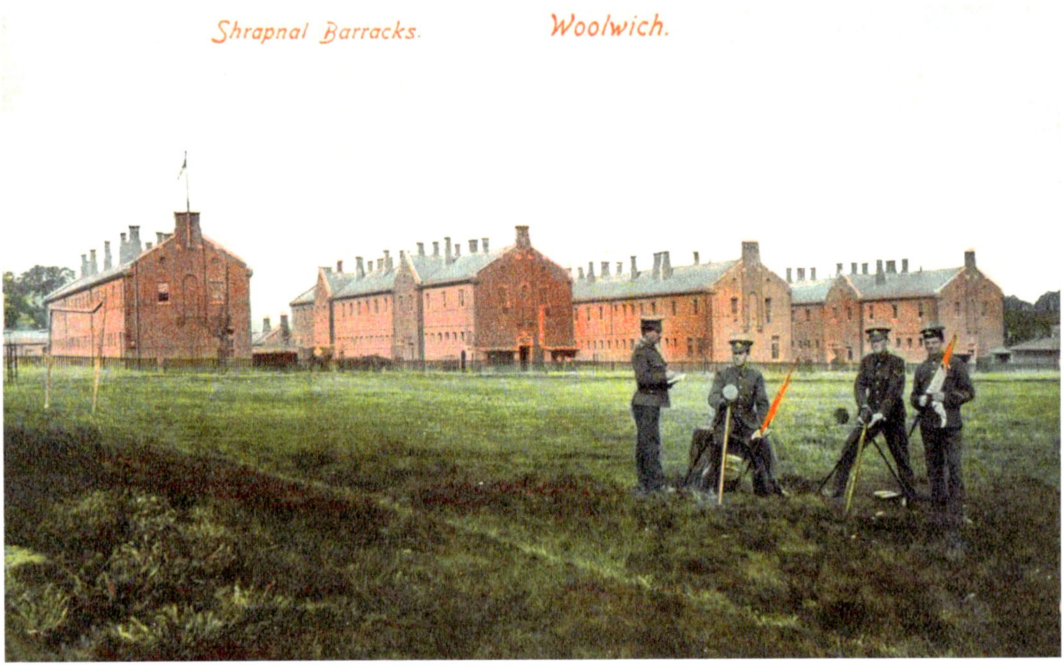


Shrapnel Barracks, *c.* 1800, named after Lt General Henry Shrapnel, shrapnel shell inventor.

Barracks, Shrapnel Barracks, Connaught Barracks, Grand Depot Barracks, Artificers Barracks, Engineer Barracks, Royal Marine Barracks, and Red Barracks.

At the Royal Academy for officers, and on the parade grounds across Woolwich, military personnel were trained to serve their country in defending and securing British global interests, embarking on ships from the dockyard in support of the many expeditions, conflicts, and wars in which Britain was engaged during the following centuries.

Regiments from Woolwich have been despatched to conflicts across Europe and beyond, including: the War of Spanish Succession (1717–14); the American Revolutionary War of Independence (1792–1802); the French Revolutionary War (1792–1802); the Napoleonic War (1802–13); the First and Second Opium Wars (1839–42 and 1856–60); the Crimean War (1853–56); the First Indian War of Independence (1857–58); the Anglo-Zulu War (1879); the Boer War (1880–81); and the Boxer Movement (1900).

The Arsenal and barracks at Woolwich were crucial to the nation throughout the First World War and the Second World War. The Arsenal manufactured an array of arms and munitions to supply British and Commonwealth forces across the globe.

The Arsenal site was referred to as the 'Secret City' due to its size of workforce, approximately 80,000 employees at its peak, around half female workers. The site consisted of four divisions: the Royal Laboratory, devoted to experimenting and producing ammunition; the Royal Carriage Department, designing and building carriages for army and naval services; the Gun Factories, for the casting and building of guns; and the Control Department, for the storage and issue of various supplies. The barracks situated across Woolwich were also integral to the war effort, and a major hub for the

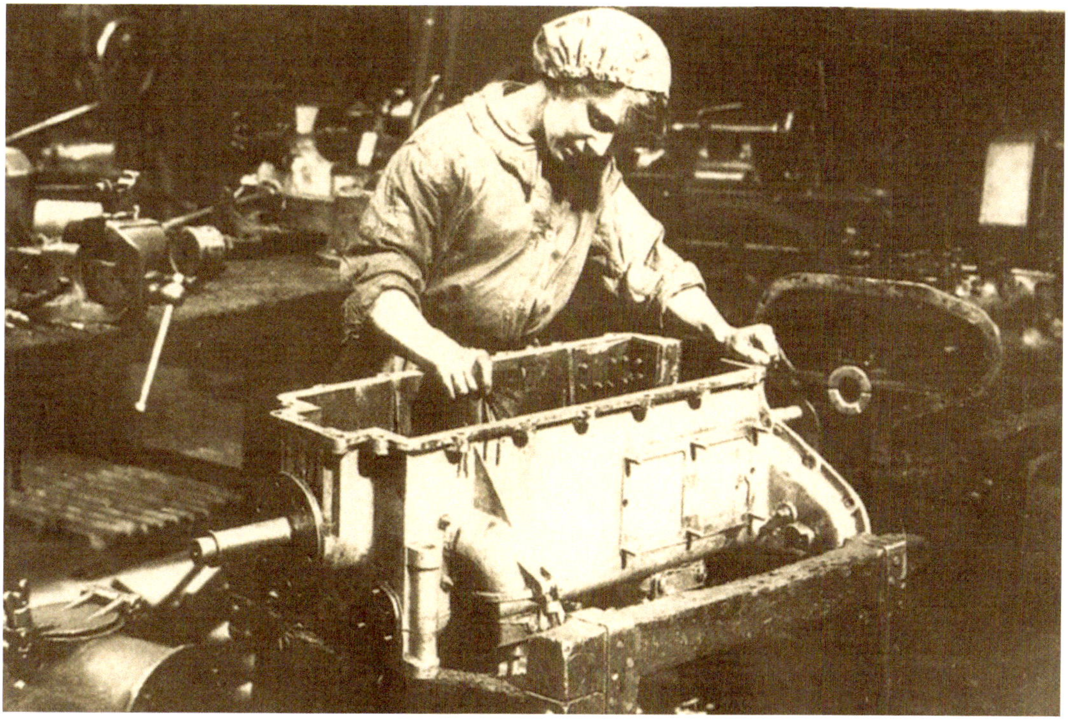

Woolwich Royal Arsenal women workers, early 1900s. (Courtesy of Greenwich Heritage Library)

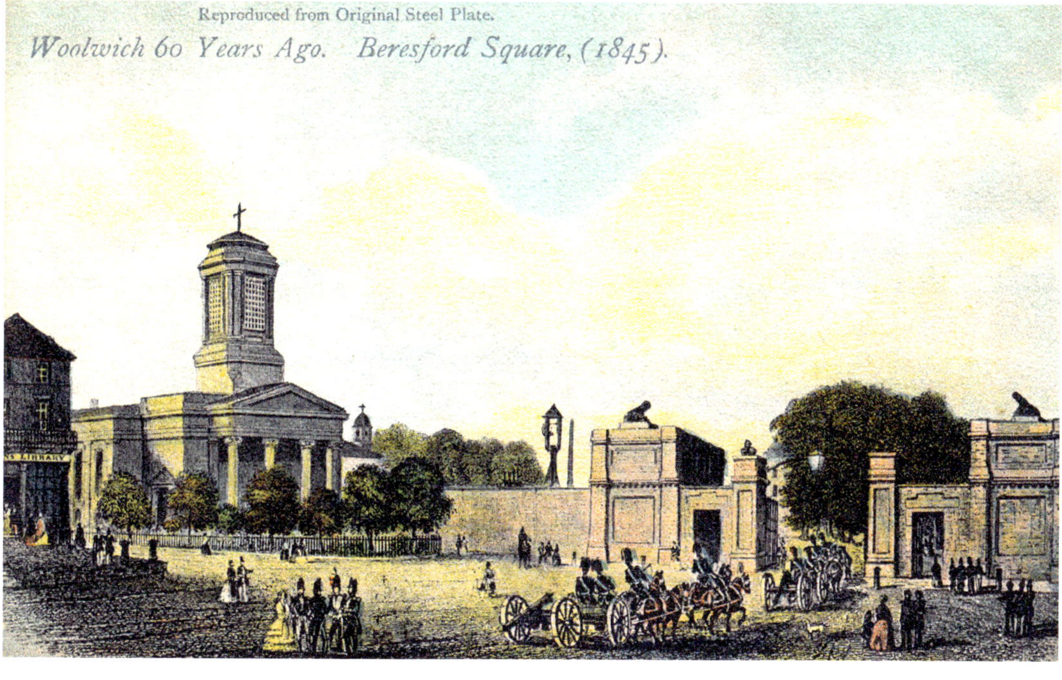


Woolwich Royal Arsenal main entrance, Beresford Square, *c.* 1845.

Royal Artillery and Royal Engineers, along with many other army units throughout both world wars. After the rescue of British forces from Dunkirk during May and June 1940, the barracks housed British forces evacuees.

Four years later, Greenwich became the key location in producing PLUTO (Pipe Line Under the Ocean), the world's very first undersea oil pipeline to supply Allied forces in France with fuel after the D-Day landings. The pipeline, a majority constructed at the Siemens Brothers site near Woolwich, was based on technology developed by Telcon at Greenwich Marsh in the production of undersea telegraph cables. The project involved laying over 700 miles of oil pipeline in great secrecy at the bottom of the English Channel.

Secrecy was paramount during the Second World War, with civilian and military efforts focused on maintaining strategic advantage over enemy forces, especially in the art of espionage.

On the outskirts of Greenwich, No. 1 Balloon Centre, RAF Station Kidbrooke, was at the very heart of British intelligence and espionage, hosting a training school for air intelligence, escape, and evasion, as well as intelligence analysis and air intelligence for Bomber Command and actions in East Asia.

Established as a Royal Flying Corps storage depot in 1917, during the Second World War a team from Kidbrooke RAF Telegraph and Wireless School developed a cypher machine known as TypeX, a superior British version of the German Enigma, for sending coded messages to military operatives and spies overseas. Between 1949 and 1953, at the height of the Cold War, the Joint Services School for Linguistics taught servicemen and servicewomen Russian, with successful graduates having the opportunity to progress on to an interrogation course.

# 4. Military Personalities

Although Greenwich has had a military presence since the pre-Roman period, it would not be until the eighth century that the riverside hamlet had its first association with a significant military commander, and self-styled King of the Anglo-Saxons.

## Alfred the Great

Alfred the Great inherited the manor of Grenewic in AD 849, when acceding his brother Aethelred to become King of Wessex, and the riverside hamlet was then included within the Anglo-Saxon kingdom of Wessex.

Alfred spent many years battling against Danish occupation, and after expelling them from London, proclaimed himself King of the Anglo-Saxons. Greenwich and large areas of surrounding land were passed down to Alfred's youngest daughter, Aelfthryth, and although Greenwich was later gifted to St Peter's Abbey in Ghent, Anglo-Saxon kings held court at the manor up to the reign of Edward I.

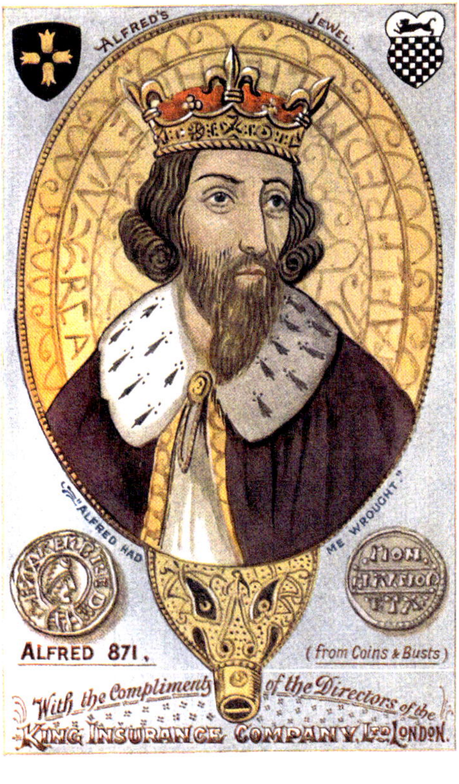


Alfred the Great, AD 848–99.

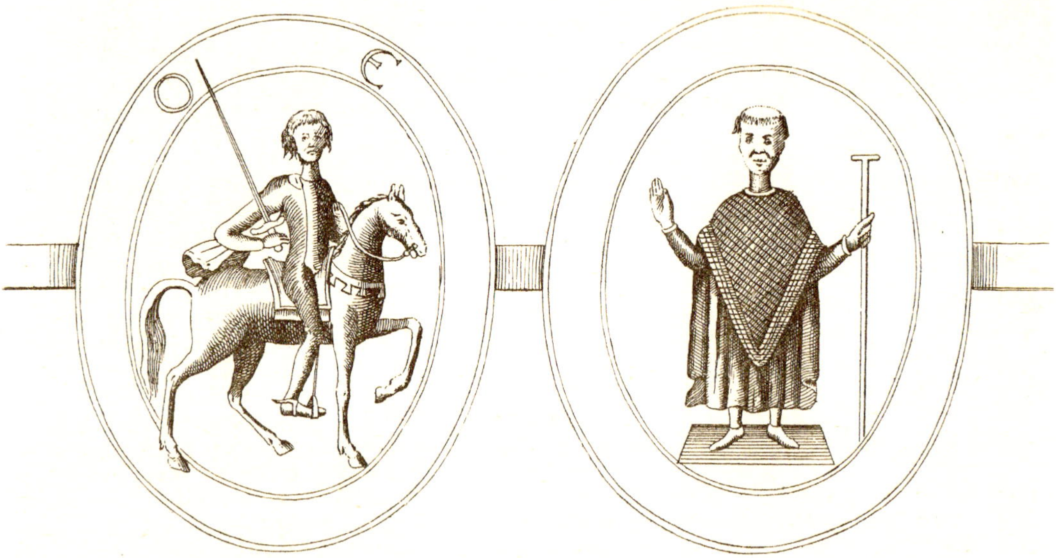

THE SEAL OF ODO, BISHOP OF BAYEUX, HALF-BROTHER OF WILLIAM I.
*Archæologia*, vol. i.

Bishop Odo, 1035–97.

## Bishop Odo of Bayeux

Following William the Conqueror's victory over the Anglo-Saxons in 1066, bishop of war Odo of Bayeux, half-brother to William, was granted the position of Earl of Kent and tenant-in-chief at the manor of Greenwich. A grange was built at Greenwich, later known as Old Court, from where the manor was administered.

Odo served as regent of England when William was absent from the country, the bishop commanding the king's forces to put down Anglo-Saxon uprisings and rebellions. When Odo fell out of favour with William, the bishop accused of oppressive misgovernment and attempting to purchase the papacy, Odo was imprisoned and his landholdings, including Greenwich, were seized by the crown.

## Humphrey, Duke of Gloucester

Acquiring the manor of Greenwich from his uncle Thomas Beaufort, Humphrey, Duke of Gloucester, younger brother of Henry V, was a well-renowned campaign commander, participating in the Hundred Years' War in France, the Battle of Agincourt and the conquest of Normandy. Enclosing 200 acres of parkland for royal hunting parties, Humphrey erected a high fortified tower at its centre, known as Greenwich Castle, as well as building a large riverside property, Bella Court, later transformed into the Palace of Placentia.

Following his brother's death, Humphrey functioned as Lord Protector of England in the government of the infant Henry VI. Falling out of favour with the king and his ministers, when Henry was old enough to rule independently, Humphrey died while imprisoned.

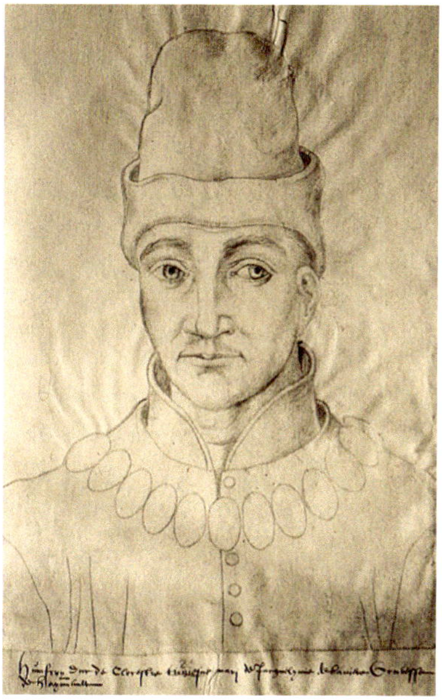

Humphrey of Lancaster, Duke of Gloucester, 1390–1447.

## Henry VII

Returning to England after spending fourteen years in exile, Henry Tudor fought to seize the crown from Richard III at the Battle of Bosworth and, following the victory, held court at the Palace of Placentia, which he had enlarged and faced with red brickwork. Spending much of his reign at Greenwich, Henry faced various rebellions and claimants

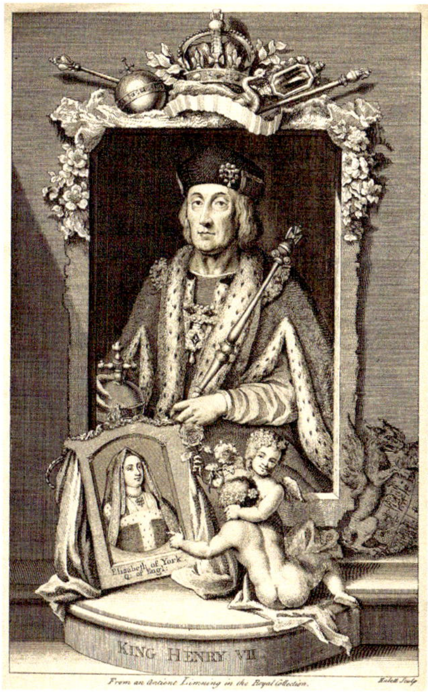


Henry VII, 1457–1509. (Courtesy of the Wellcome Collection)

to the throne, it has also been speculated that the king may have been involved in the murder of the Princes in the Tower.

From Greenwich, Henry made plans to expand royal shipbuilding and invested in the nearby dockyard at Deptford. After Henry VII's youngest son, Henry, ascended to the throne in 1509, he furthered his father's plans to increase the size of the naval force.

## Henry VIII

Born at Greenwich Palace in June 1491, Henry was baptised at the nearby Church of the Observant Franciscans. After the death of his older brother, Arthur, Henry was betrothed to his sibling's widow, Catherine of Aragon, and after marriage they spent most of their married years holding court at the palace.

Henry created the Navy Board, an administrative naval wing to oversee the running of naval forces, and the king's warships now carried heavier guns and watertight gunports, an advancement in naval warfare. In 1543, the Treaty of Greenwich was signed between English and Scottish representatives to unite both kingdoms and seal the peace with the betrothal of Henry's son, Edward, to Mary, Queen of Scots, but the treaty was rejected by the Scottish parliament.

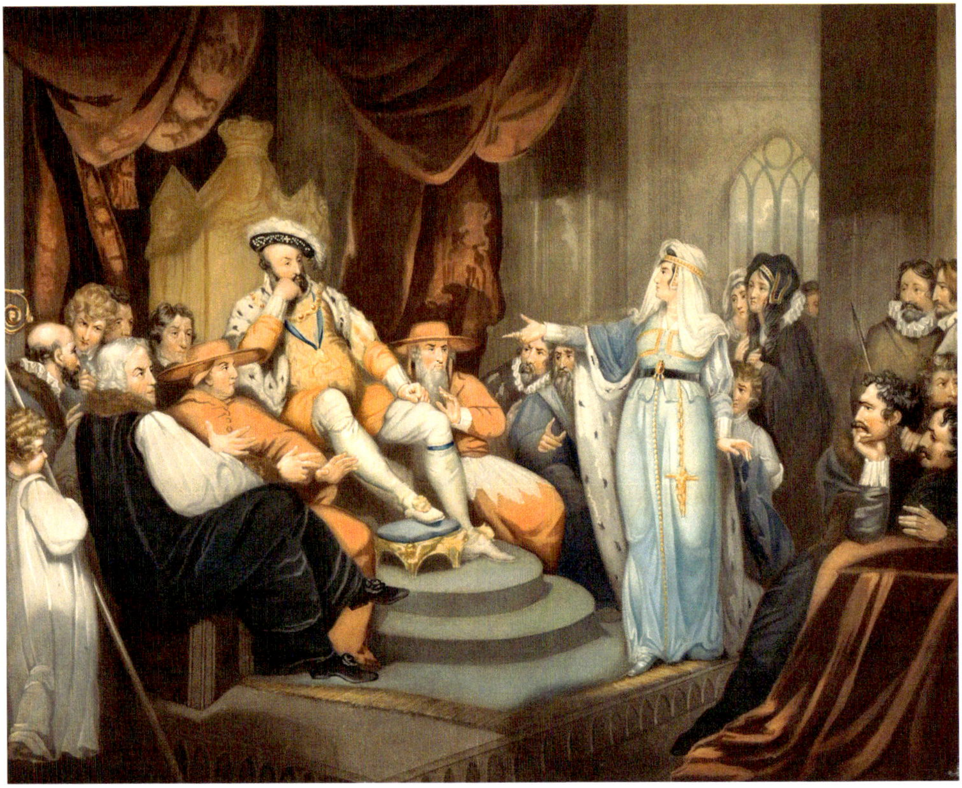

Henry VIII, 1491–1547. (Courtesy of the Wellcome Collection)

## Edward VI

Henry was succeeded in 1547 by his only legitimate son, nine-year-old Edward, and although his reign was brief, the realm governed by a regency council; militarily, it was eventful. Edward and his council were faced with economic difficulties and social discontent, which broke out in rebellion and riots, resulting in the introduction of martial law and an expensive war with Scotland, which eventually ended with military withdrawal.

In January 1553, Edward fell ill and returned from Westminster to Greenwich. Large crowds arrived with the expectation of seeing the king. After making an appearance at the palace window, Edward's health deteriorated. Nearing death, it is believed Edward willed his cousin Lady Jayne Grey to succeed him, Edward passing away at Greenwich during July 1553, aged just fifteen. The mayor of London and several city officials were summoned to pledge allegiance to Edward's cousin, who reigned at Greenwich Palace for nine days before being deposed by city officials in favour of Mary Tudor who had raised support for her claim to the throne. Lady Jane Grey was executed by beheading in February 1554.

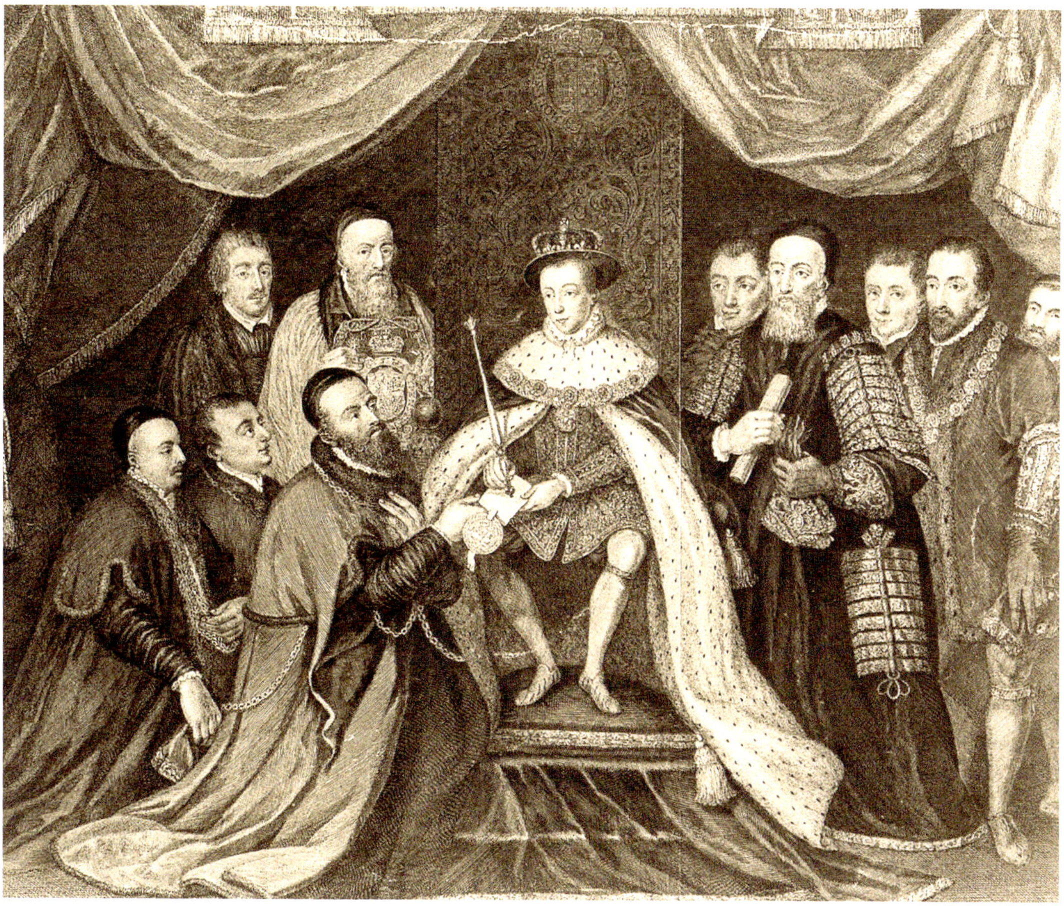

Edward VI 1537–53. (Courtesy of the Wellcome Collection)

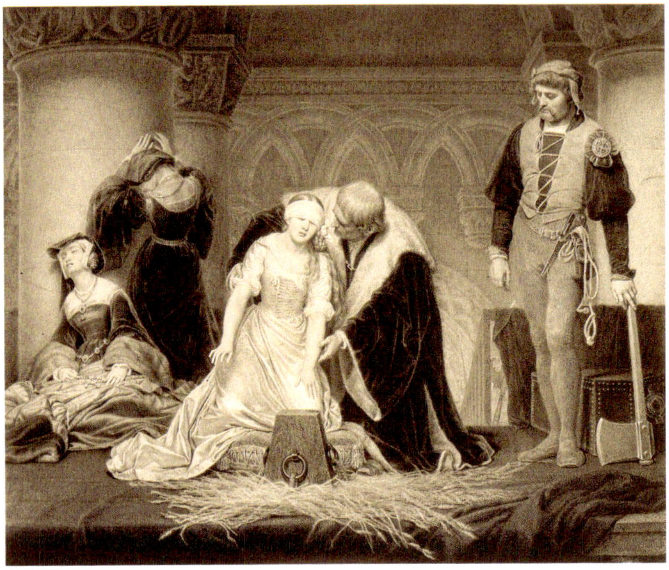

Lady Jane Grey, 1537–54. (Courtesy of the Wellcome Collection)

## Mary I

Mary Tudor reigned from 1553 to 1558, and Greenwich Palace played a significant part in the early years of Mary's life, especially during the reign of her father, Henry VIII. At Greenwich, where Mary was born, the young princess received education in languages, music, dance, and religious studies, and while at Greenwich was allowed to practise Catholicism.

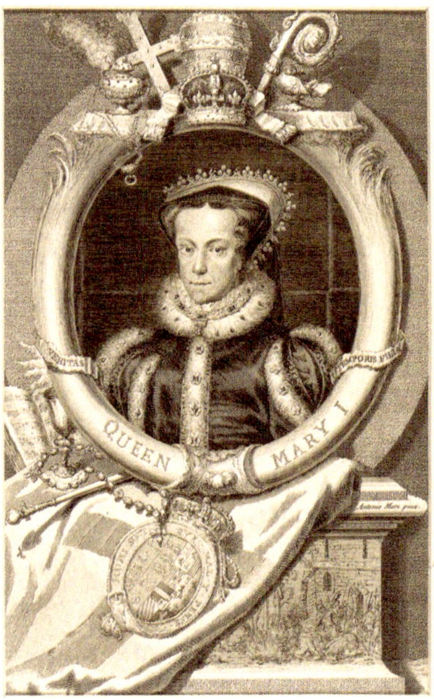


Mary I, 1516–58. (Courtesy of the Wellcome Collection)

Mary's reign was marked by violent armed campaigns against her Protestant subjects, where hundreds were rounded up by the queen's militia to be burned at the stake, earning her the name 'Bloody Mary'. Greenwich remained an important royal residence during her bloody reign holding court at the palace marked by a series of political and religious hostilities.

## Elizabeth I

Born at Greenwich Palace in 1533, Elizabeth Tudor was crowned queen after the death of her sister Mary, making the palace a main royal residence and principal seat of court following her coronation.

After the English fleet's victory over the Spanish, a parade was held at Greenwich Palace to display captured Spanish treasures, and a scaled-down re-enactment of the Spanish Armada's defeat took place on the Thames off Deptford Dockyard in 1560. In response to threats from Catholic conspirators, Elizabeth held a grand military review in Greenwich Park, where a complement of 1,400 men-at-arms gathered as a show of force against the plotters, including her cousin Mary, Queen of Scots. Eventually, Mary was arrested and charged with treason, Elizabeth reluctantly signing her death warrant while holding court at Greenwich.

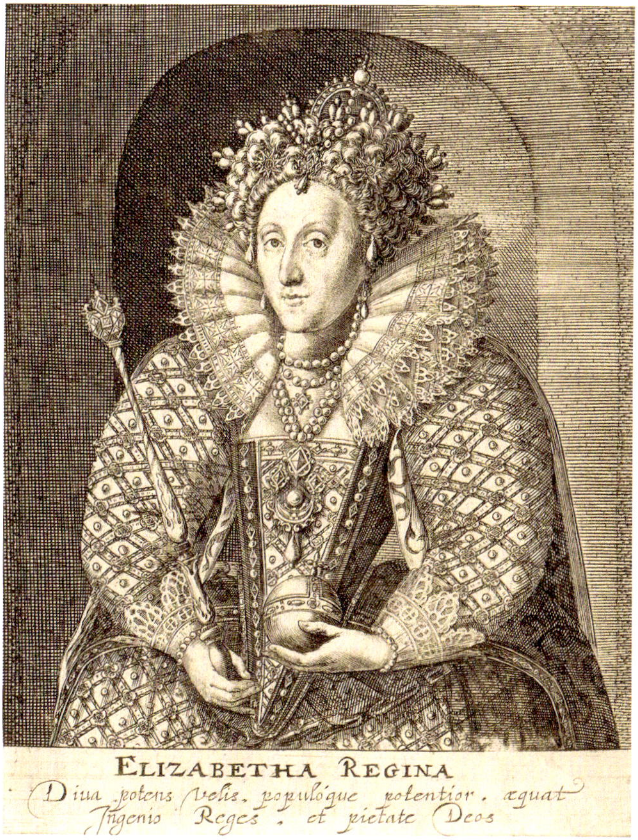


Elizabeth I, 1533–1603. (Courtesy of the Wellcome Collection)

## James I

Scottish King James VI, son of Mary, Queen of Scots, ascended to the English throne after Elizabeth's death, moving the royal court from Scotland to Greenwich Palace, away from the capital of London, but close to the Royal Dockyards.

Surviving conspiracies to remove him from the throne, including a plot by Catholic conspirators to blow up the king and the government in Parliament House, James's reign was relatively peaceful, becoming known as 'Rex Pacificus' or 'Peacemaker King'. Nevertheless, the marriage alliances James arranged with peace in mind inadvertently led to the outbreak of the Thirty Years' War, when Fredrick of Palatinate, the king's son-in-law, promised to support bringing down Catholic Habsburg power throughout Germany. For the final six years of James's reign, a renewal of Protestant and Catholic conflict broke out across Europe.

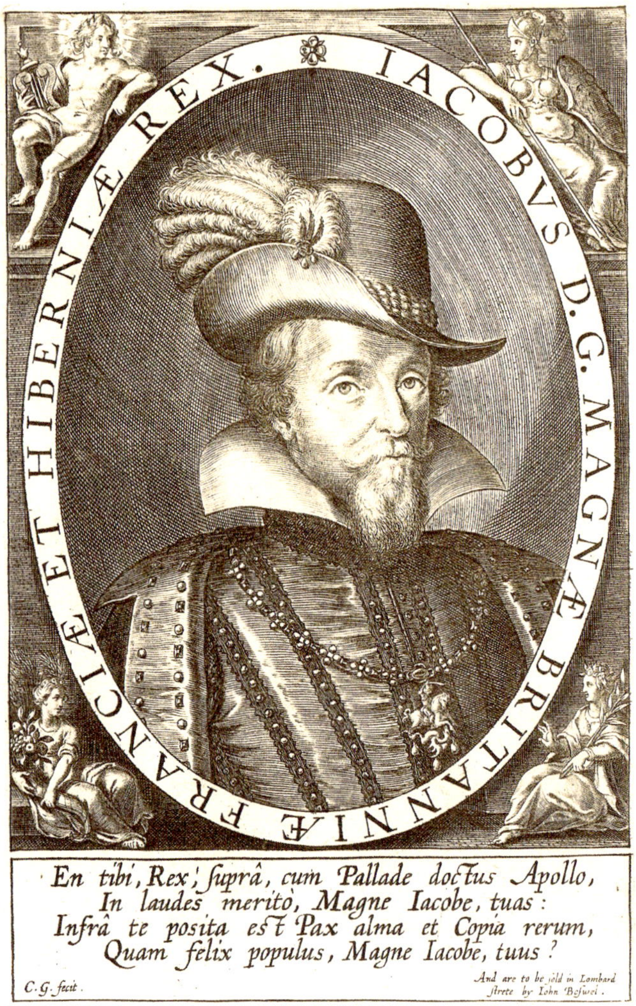


James VI and I, 1566–1625. (Courtesy of the Wellcome Collection)

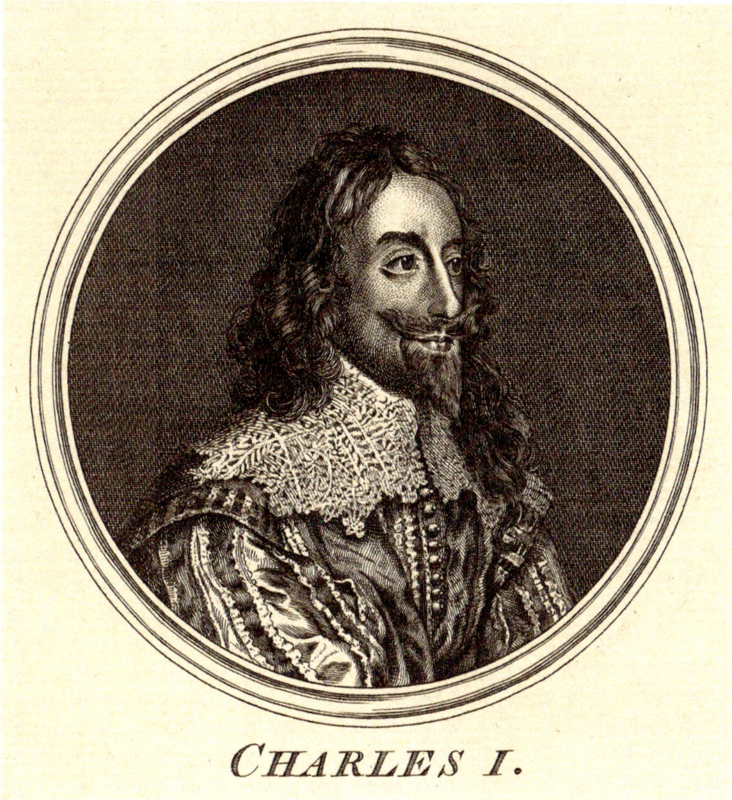


Charles I, 1600–49. (Courtesy of the Wellcome Collection)

## Charles I

Ascending to the throne in 1625, James's son Charles held court at Greenwich Palace and enjoyed spending time there with his wife, Henrietta Maria, where the king held extravagant entertainments and went hunting deer in the park. Charles I was constantly in contention with Parliament, which had attempted to curb his royal privileges and spending.

The king was determined to govern as he saw fit, including raising taxes without Parliamentary consent, which many subjects opposed, and civil war eventually broke out between the Royalists and Parliamentarians. With the forces of the Parliamentarians closing in on Charles, the king made his escape from Greenwich Palace shortly before the royal residence was searched.

## Oliver Cromwell

After the defeat of the Royalists, culminating in the execution of Charles I, charged and found guilty of treason, Greenwich Palace was given over for the use of the Lord Protector and senior commander of the Parliamentarian army, Oliver Cromwell.

Cromwell attempted to sell the palace and park, but to no avail, so he used the palace buildings as a biscuit factory to supply the army, then briefly as a camp for Dutch prisoners of war. After this, the palace was left vacant and in a poor state of repair.

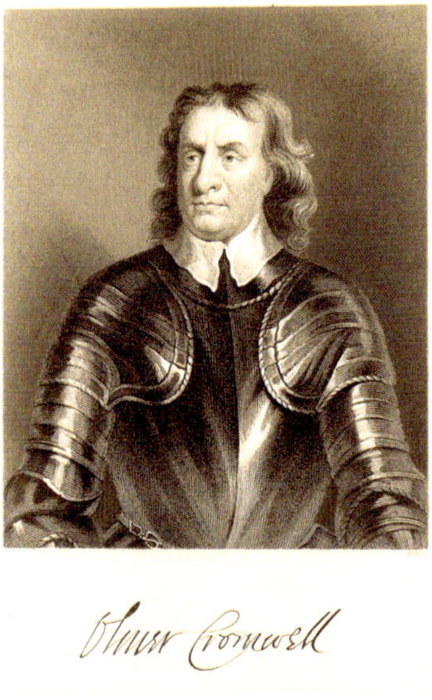


Oliver Cromwell, 1599–1658. (Courtesy of the Wellcome Collection)

## Charles II

On the Restoration of the Monarchy, Charles II returned to hold court at Greenwich. After nine years living in exile on the Continent, the king found many of the minor royal residences had either been sold or destroyed, the larger palaces fallen to ruin, and although Greenwich Palace was in a poor condition, it was the most habitable.

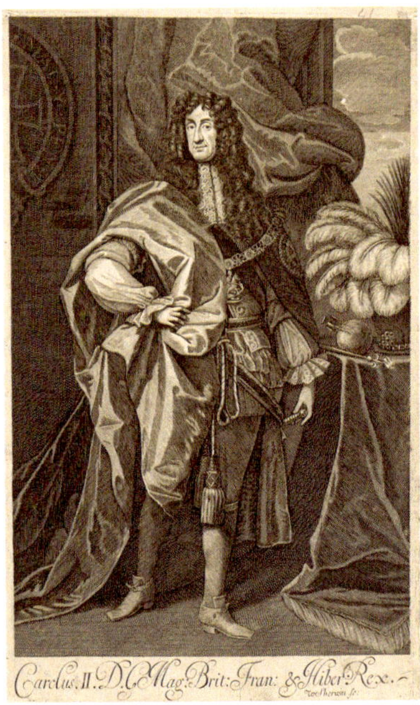


Charles II, 1630–85. (Courtesy of the Wellcome Collection)

Charles not only set about restoring the palace, but the king also raised a force of 5,000 men-at-arms, known as the King's Guards and the King's Troop of Horse Guards, later known as the Life Guards, along with a former Royalist regiment which became the Coldstream Guards. After plague struck London, followed by the Great Fire, Charles's attention turned to rebuilding the city rather than constructing a new palace at Greenwich.

## Samuel Pepys

One who witnessed both the plague and the Great Fire of London was Samuel Pepys, who travelled on the ship with Charles II on his return from exile. Pepys was appointed Clerk of the Acts to the Navy Board, the diarist responsible for the administration of the Royal Navy.

Pepys took up office at Deptford Dockyard, from where he supervised the overhaul of the navy, setting higher standards in ship design, improving conditions and pay for crews, and creating mathematical and navigation exams for officers. The need for a mathematical and scientific approach to ship navigation accuracy culminated in the building of the Greenwich Royal Observatory.

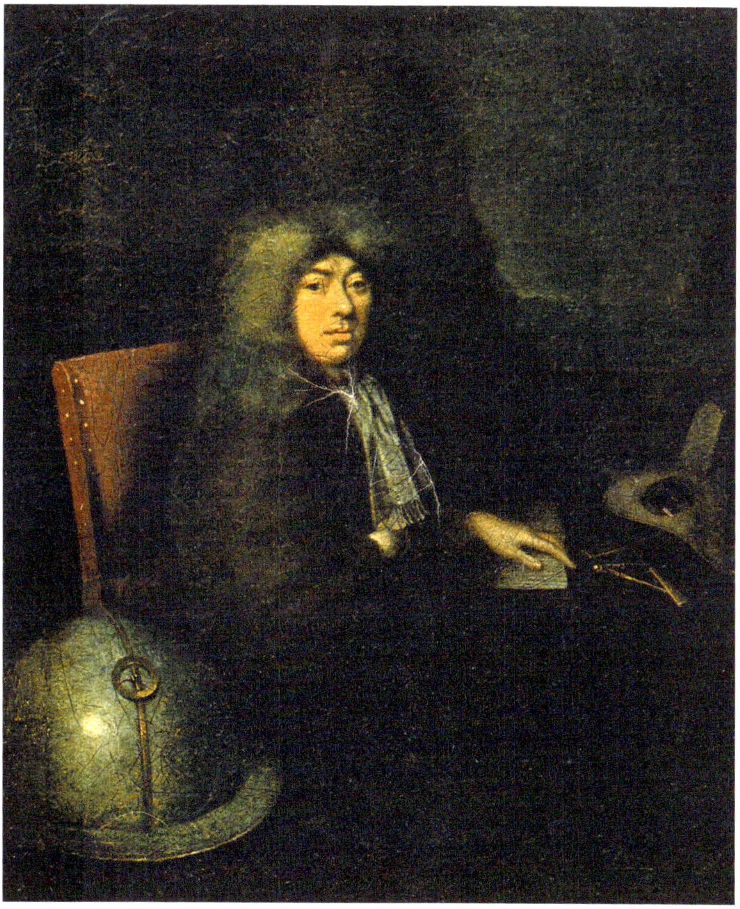

Samuel Pepys 1633–1703. (Courtesy of the Wellcome Collection)

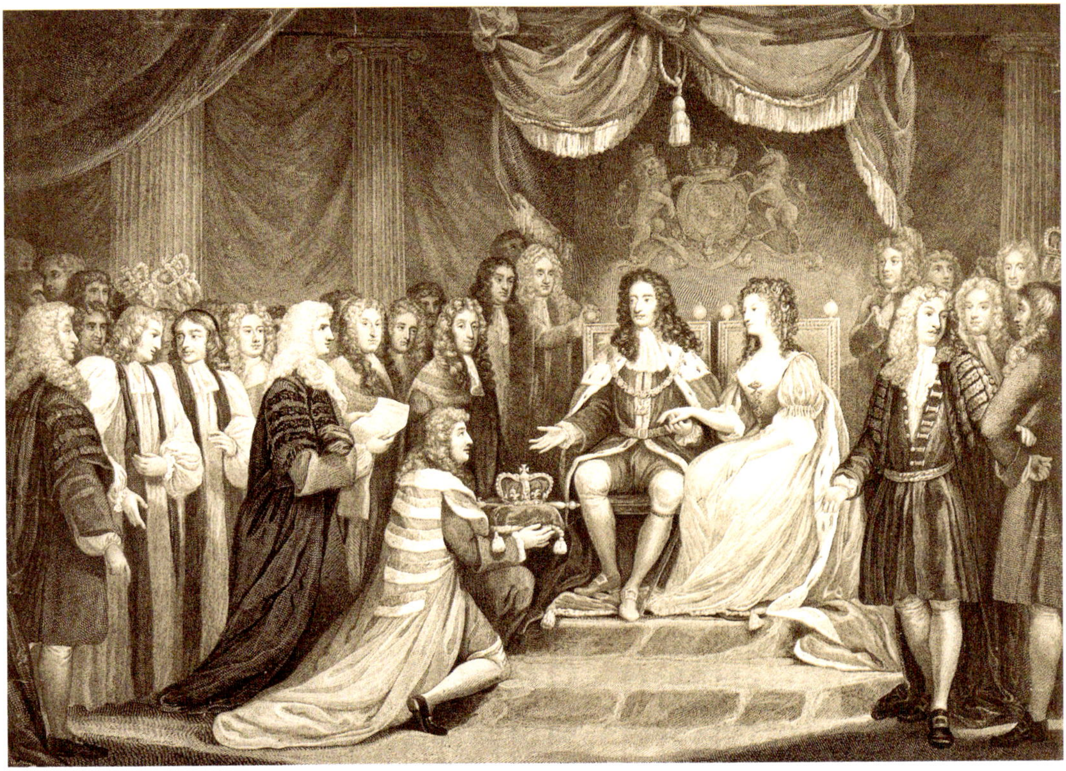

William III, 1650–1702, and Mary II, 1662–94. (Courtesy of the Wellcome Collection)

## William and Mary

After the death of Charles II, the king was succeeded by his younger brother James; however, unpopular because of his Catholic views, the king was forced to abdicate in favour of his daughter Mary and her husband, William of Orange. Although first taking up royal residence at the Queen's House, along with the only wing completed of Charles II's ambitiously planned new Greenwich Palace adjacent, Mary preferred residing at other available royal houses.

Following the naval battle of La Hogue, where Royal Navy crews suffered terrible injuries, Mary donated the unfinished Charles II wing for use as a hospital and refuge for injured and retired seamen, along similar lines to the hospital for retired military at Chelsea, some of the funding going towards its construction coming from seized proceeds of suspected pirate Captain Kidd.

## Greenwich Pensioners

The first Greenwich Pensioners arrived in 1705, either injured or retired, with some fallen on hard times, referred to as 'Greenwich Geese' by locals for their rowdy behaviour. Life at sea during the age of sail was an extremely dangerous occupation, where accidents and disease were more common than suffering injuries through conflict. Pensioners were housed in small cells, a room with a bunk, desk, and storage for their uniform, which

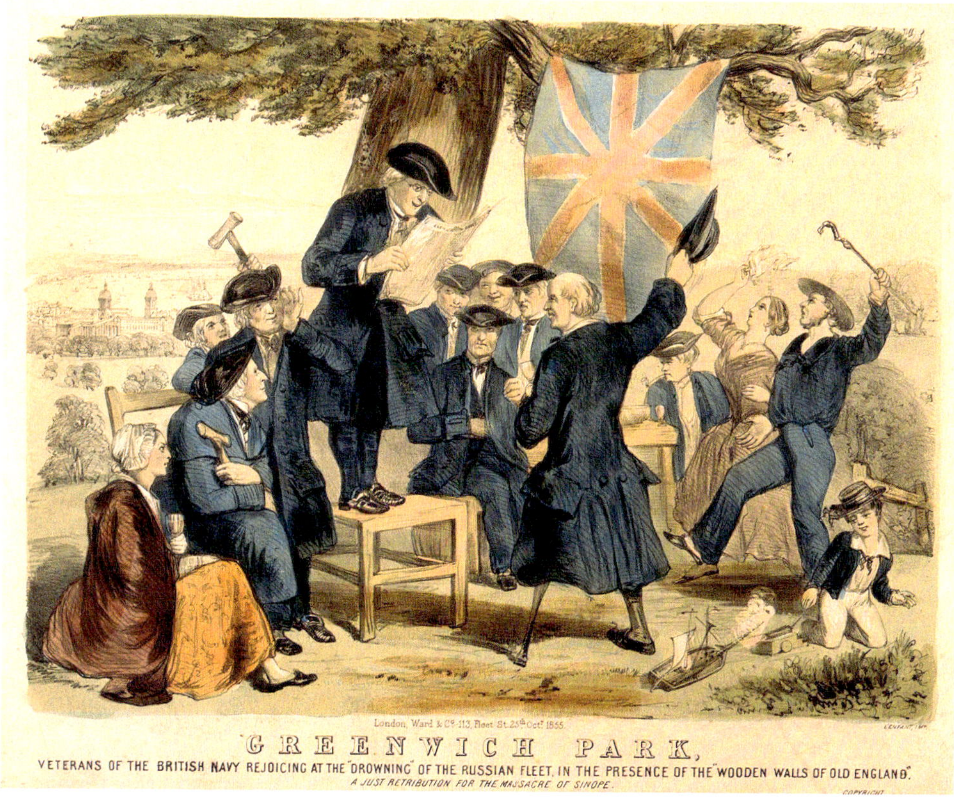


Greenwich pensioners, residents from 1705 to 1869. (Courtesy of the Wellcome Collection)

consisted of a traditional black tricorne hat, a yellow-lined dark blue frock coat, white britches, and stockings.

Required to earn their keep by conducting various chores, pensioners were often out frequenting local inns and beerhouses, recalling adventures at sea in exchange for a tankard of beer or tot of rum. However, pensioners' conduct was carefully scrutinised. Punishments for drunkenness or bad behaviour included confinement to premises on a diet of bread and water, and the humiliation of being ordered to wear their frock coat inside out to show the yellow lining.

## James Wolfe

Son of the distinguished General Edward Wolfe, James Wolfe relocated with his family to Greenwich from Westerham. Joining up with his father's regiment as a volunteer at thirteen years old, Wolfe then received a commission as second lieutenant in the marines. Transferred to the British Army infantry, Wolfe rose swiftly through the ranks. Leading his regiment into action against the Jacobite army of Bonnie Prince Charlie at the battles of Falkirk and Culloden, Wolfe came to fame for refusing direct orders to shoot dead a wounded Highlander, exclaiming he would rather resign his post than sacrifice his honour.

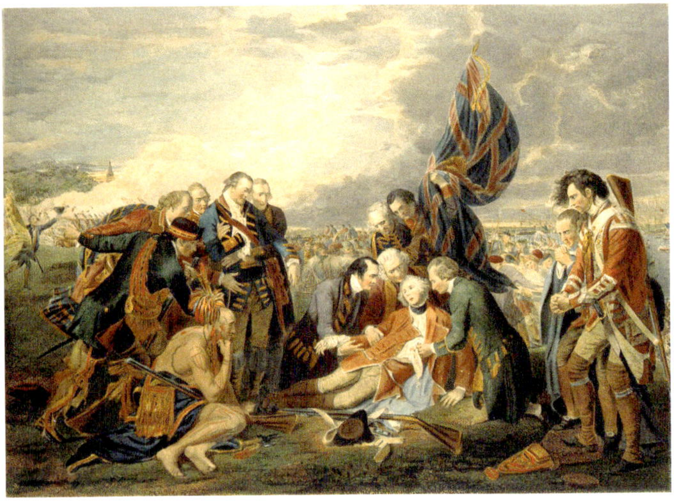

Major General James Wolfe, 1727–59. (Courtesy of the Wellcome Collection)

At the age of twenty-three, Wolfe attained the rank of major general during the Seven Years' War with France. Commanding a surprise assault on French-held Quebec on 13 September 1759, the French capitulated after fifteen minutes of action. Wolfe was mortally wounded during the battle, saying as he lay dying, 'Now, God be praised, I will die in peace.' Wolfe's defeat of the French led to the capture of French-held Canada and the eventual creation of Canada as a nation. The body of the hero of Quebec was brought home for internment in the family vault at St Alfege Church.

## Horatio Nelson

The most famous Royal Navy admiral, Horatio Nelson, spent some time convalescing at the Royal Hospital after suffering a bout of malaria while serving aboard HMS *Seahorse*

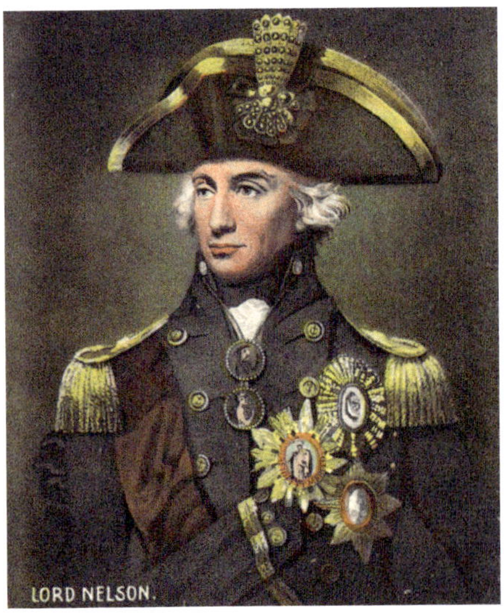


Horatio Nelson, 1st Viscount Nelson, 1st Duke of Bronte, 1758–1805.

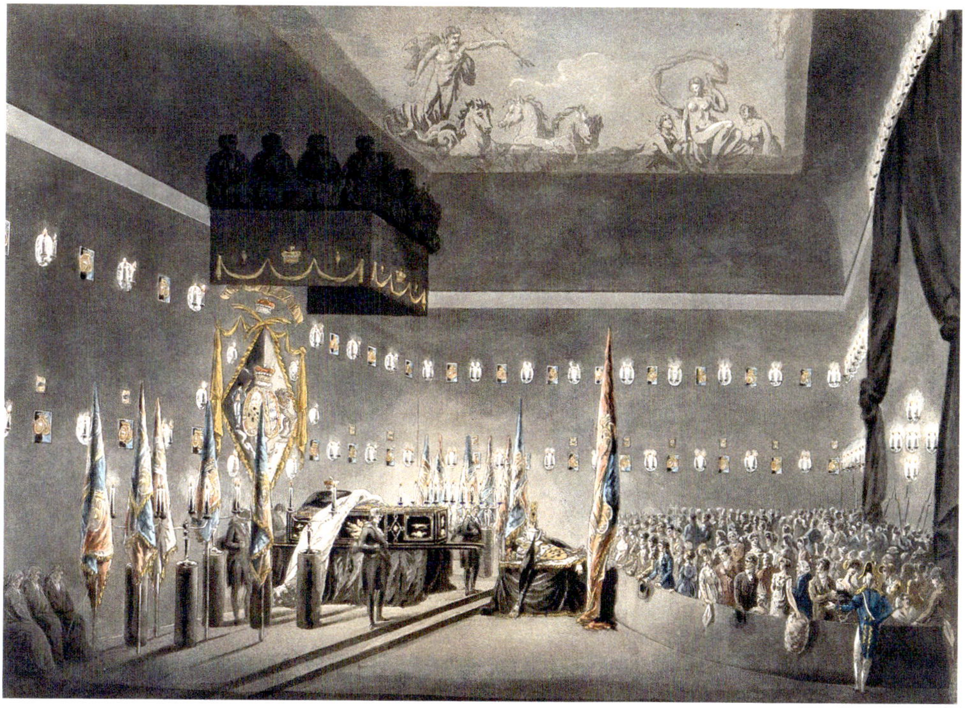

Lord Nelson lying in state, Painted Hall, Greenwich Hospital, 5–7 January 1806. (Courtesy of the Wellcome Collection)

in Asia, then again after losing his right arm commanding an attempted amphibious landing from HMS *Theseus* during a battle at Santa Cruz.

Born in Norfolk, Nelson joined the navy as an ordinary seaman, gaining promotions through his many exploits at sea. During the Battle of Trafalgar, Nelson was shot by a sniper and died aboard his flagship HMS *Victory*, but not before the battle was won. On Christmas Eve 1805, the body of Nelson arrived at Greenwich Hospital, where he lay in state for three days in the Painted Hall before transported by river procession for interment at St Paul's Cathedral. The uniform Nelson wore when he was shot is now exhibited in the National Maritime Museum.

## Louis Napoléon Bonaparte

The last in succession to the French throne, Prince Imperial Louis Napoléon Bonaparte, joined the British Army and graduated from the Royal Military Academy at Woolwich after the French royal family had been exiled to England, taking up residence at Chislehurst. Attached to the Royal Artillery, the young prince requested a posting to Africa, anticipating taking part in the Anglo-Zulu War.

His superiors reluctantly gave permission, and the Prince Imperial was dispatched to join the staff of the commander in South Africa. In June 1879, the Prince Imperial took command of a reconnaissance party entering deep into Zulu-held territory, where they were ambushed by Zulu skirmishers. Mortally wounded, the Prince Imperial's body was

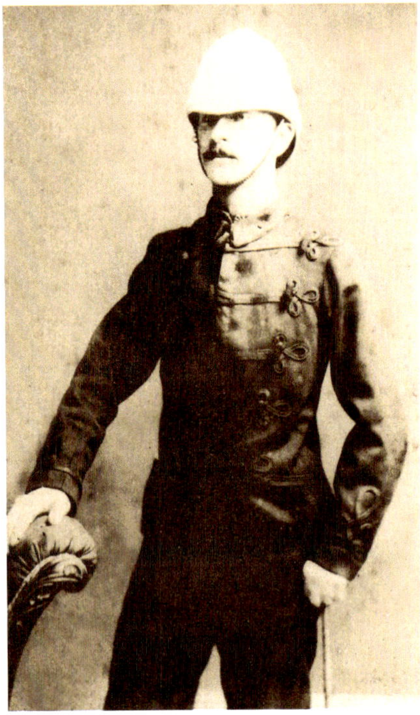

Prince Imperial, Louis-Napoléon Bonaparte, 1856–79.

later recovered, his remains returned to the Royal Arsenal and placed temporarily within a riverside guardhouse, which functioned as a mortuary, until transported in procession to Chislehurst, attended by Queen Victoria.

## General Charles George Gordon

Known through his exploits as 'Chinese Gordon', 'Gordon of Pasha', and 'Gordon of Khartoum', Charles George Gordon was born in Woolwich in January 1833, serving in the British Army between 1852 and 1885. The men of the Gordon family had served as officers over four generations, and Charles Gordon, attaining the rank of major general, was the fifth. After attending the Royal Military Academy at Woolwich, Gordon joined the Royal Engineers, seeing action in the Crimean War and, while serving in China, supported the Manchu-led dynasty during the Taiping Civil War.

With permission from the British government, Gordon was attached to serve under the Ottoman Khedive, Governor of Egypt and the Sudan, where he was active in suppressing uprisings and revolts, subduing beheadings, floggings, and slave trading. When a serious revolt broke out, the British government, unwilling to send further forces to Sudan, gave Gordon orders to evacuate civilians and British and Egyptian regiments from Khartoum after coming under attack from the forces of the self-proclaimed Mahdi.

Gordon, acting on his own initiative, decided to defend the city after evacuating civilians. When news arrived back home in Britain of Gordon's stand, the public demanded the government send a relief force, which finally arrived after General Gordon had been struck down and killed on the steps of the governor general's palace.

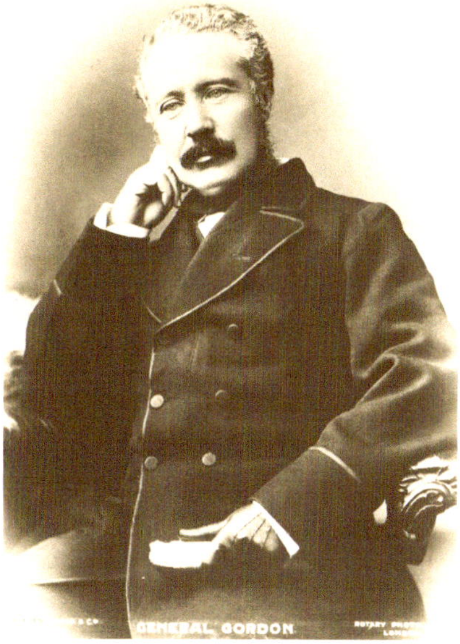


Major General Charles George Gordon, 1833–85.

## Eric Gascoigne Robinson VC

Recipient of the Victoria Cross, Eric Gascoigne Robinson of the Royal Navy, born in Greenwich in May 1882, earned his award by single-handedly destroying a Turkish gun battery during the Gallipoli campaign. Robinson's father was chaplain of the Royal Naval College. Young Robinson was destined for a career at sea, joining the crew of HMS *Britannia* at the age of fifteen.

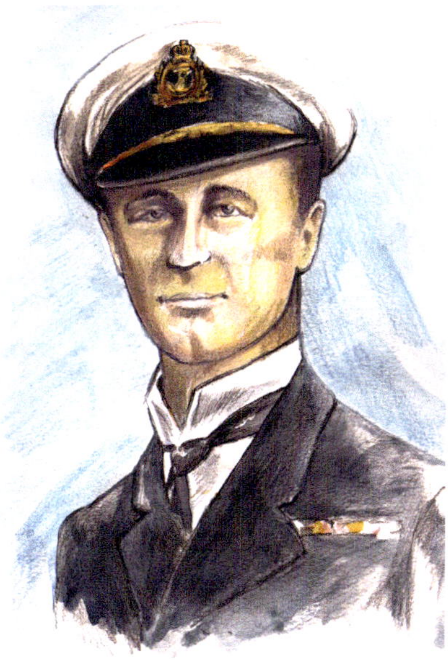

Eric Gascoigne Robinson VC, 1882–1965.

Seeing his first action while serving aboard HMS *Endymion* during the Boxer Movement in north China, Robinson, wounded while part of a relief force, was mentioned in despatches for his reputation as a daring and resourceful officer. After the action in Gallipoli, which earned Robinson the Victoria Cross, he also volunteered to destroy the stranded submarine HMS *E15*, which was captured by Turkish forces. In command of two torpedo-armed picket boats, Robinson was successful in completing the mission.

Posted to the Caspian Sea after the end of the First World War as part of an Allied intervention during the Russian Civil War, Robinson commanded twelve armed Coastal Motor Boats. Robinson's first action was in forcing vessels of the Centro-Caspian Flotilla to surrender; he then later led the Coastal Motor Boat squadron in an attack on the harbour of Bolshevik-held Fort Alexandrovsky, resulting in the garrison's surrender. Attaining the rank of rear admiral, Robinson commanded convoys across the Atlantic during the Second World War.

## Cecil Sewell VC

One of nine children, Greenwich-born Cecil Sewell's family resided at a house on Crooms Hill, west Greenwich. At the outbreak of the First World War, Sewell enlisted in the British Army, rising to the rank of lieutenant in the Queen's Own Royal West Kent Regiment, attached to the 3rd Light Battalion Tank Corps.

Heading towards the final months of the war, at Frémicourt in France, Sewell, while commanding a section of Whippet tanks and under heavy fire, left his own tank to go to the aid of a crew whose tank had overturned and caught fire. Releasing the men trapped inside, Sewell saw one of his own crew lying wounded on the ground. He was hit by gunfire while returning to his tank across open ground but continued onwards. Attending to his wounded tank driver, Sewell was hit again and killed on 29 August 1918, aged twenty-three. For his outstanding act of bravery, Sewell received the Victoria Cross.

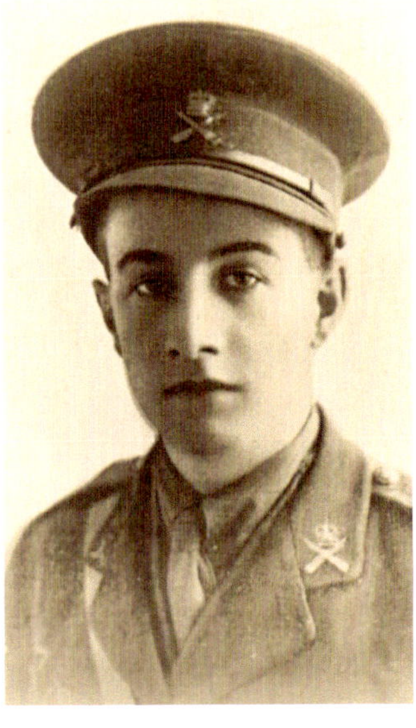

Cecil Harold Sewell VC, 1895–1918.

## Jack Rose

One of very few RAF pilots who survived from the first day of the Second World War to the last, Jack Rose was born at Blackheath in January 1917. Educated at Shooters Hill School after studying science at University College, London, Rose joined the Royal Air Force Volunteer Reserve in 1938 to train as a fighter pilot.

Stationed in northern France during 1940, Rose flew a Hawker Hurricane, shooting down three German aircraft before the squadron was evacuated back to England. Rose then served with No. 32 Squadron based at Biggin Hill during the Battle of Britain. While flying sorties from Exeter with Czech and Polish squadrons, Rose received the Distinguished Flying Cross.

While in command of No. 184 Squadron, Rose pioneered the use of rockets fired from Hurricane bombers, the squadron making ground attacks during the D-Day landings. Rose went on to lead No. 113 Squadron in support of the Fourteenth Army's advance on Rangoon before the Japanese surrender in August 1945.

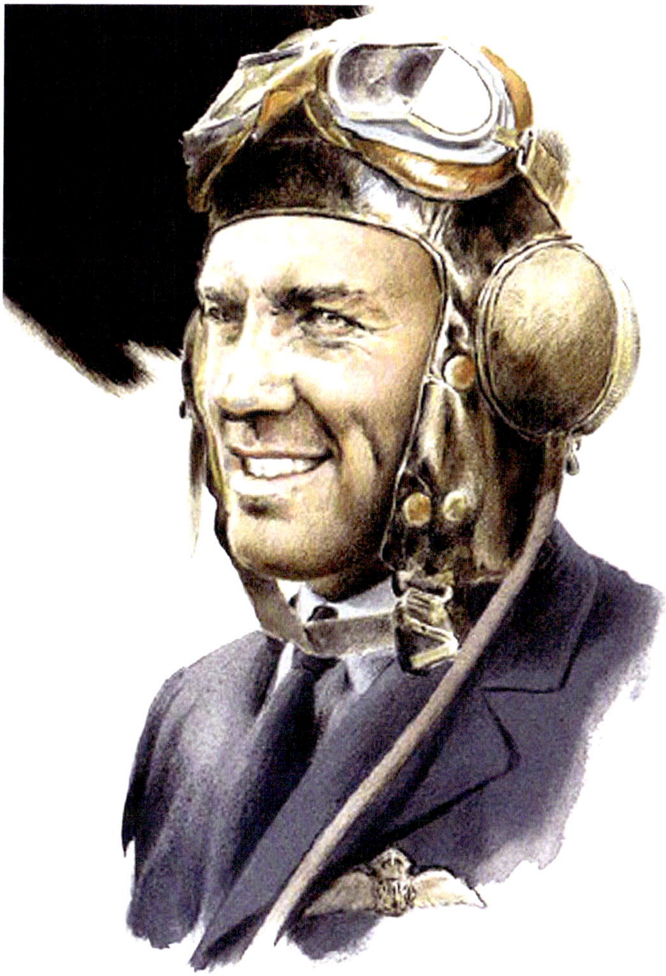

Wing Commander Jack Rose VC, 1917–2009. (Courtesy of Shoreham Aircraft Museum)

## Military Units

Through all the borough's long military past, the Royal Artillery was one of the town's most recognised units. Established at the Arsenal, the Royal Artillery regiment relocated to purpose-built barracks on Woolwich Common in 1770. Artillery had been in use during campaigns since the mid-fourteenth century, and after the Restoration of the Monarchy, John Churchill, 1st Duke of Marlborough, appointed Master-General of Ordnance, initiated a series of military reforms which divided the existing Ordnance Service into artillery and engineers.

Two field companies of artillery were formed by royal warrant and quartered in the Warren at the Arsenal site. By 1771, the Royal Regiment of Artillery numbered over 2,500 men, around a third of which quartered in Woolwich.

A cadet company was formed in 1741 to train prospective artillery and engineering officers, and to provide mobile artillery support for cavalry units. The Royal Horse Artillery was formed in 1793, along with the formation of the Corps of Royal Artillery Drivers.

During the seventeenth century, the Royal Artillery engaged in all major campaigns of the Napoleonic Wars, and when the East India Company was dissolved in 1862 their artillery was absorbed by the Royal Artillery. By 1899, the Royal Artillery comprised of three groups: the Royal Horse Artillery, the Royal Field Artillery, and the Royal Garrison

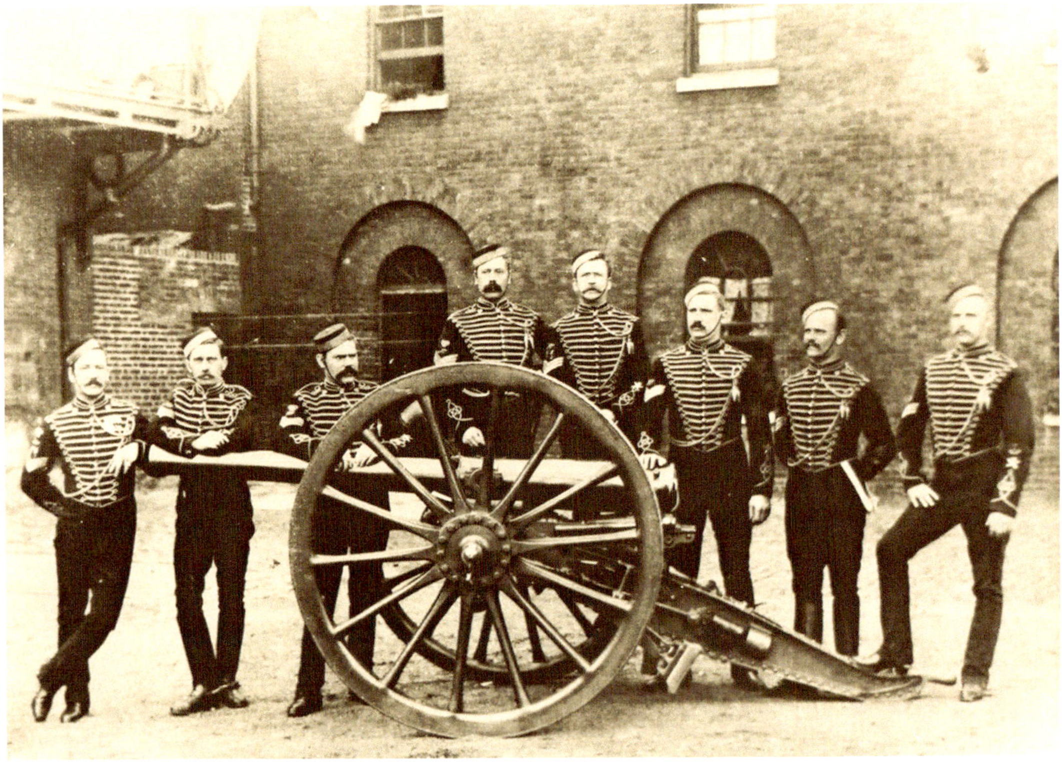

Gun unit of the Royal Regiment of Artillery, formed in 1716.

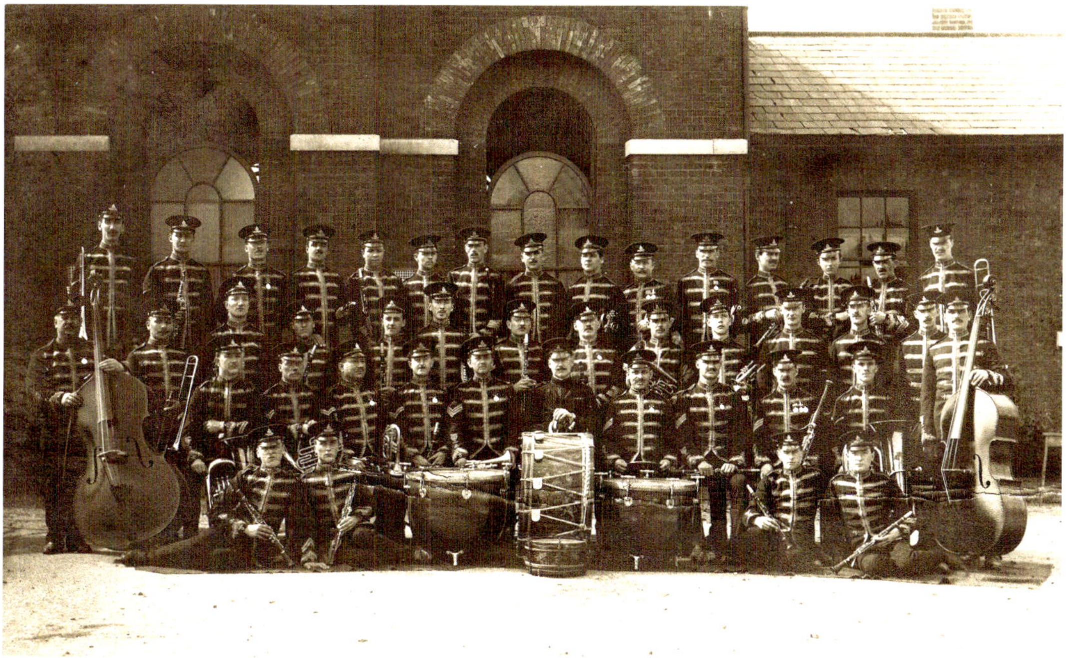

Royal Artillery Band, the first and permanent British military band, originating in 1557.

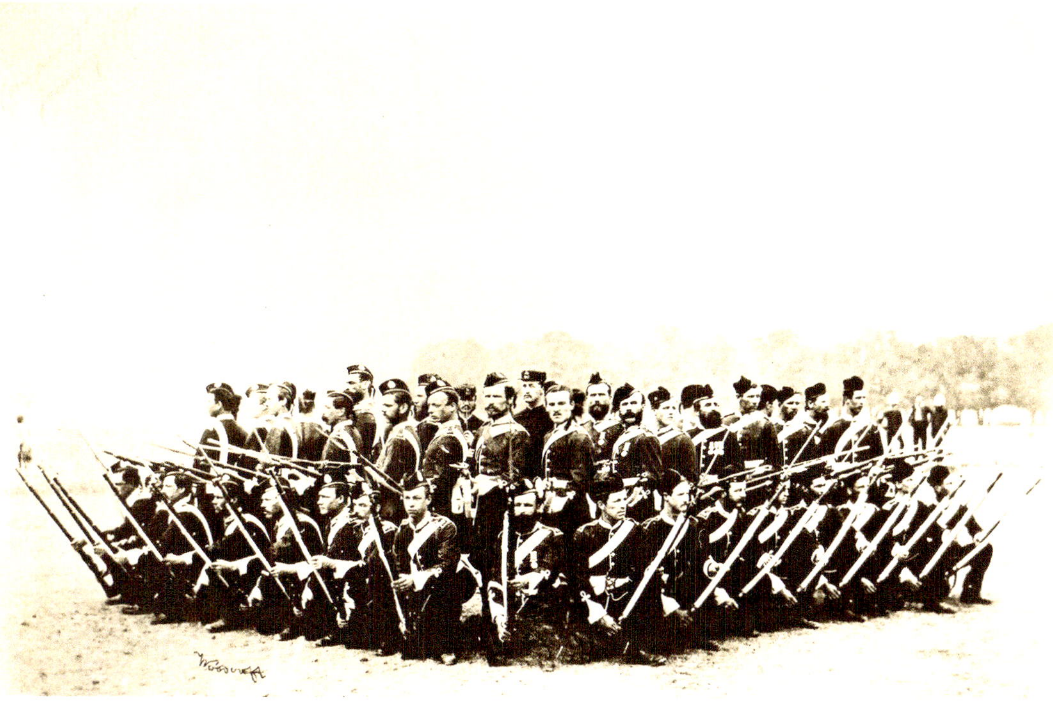

40th Foot Regiment Woolwich Common, *c.* 1894. The regiment fought under General Wolfe at Quebec.

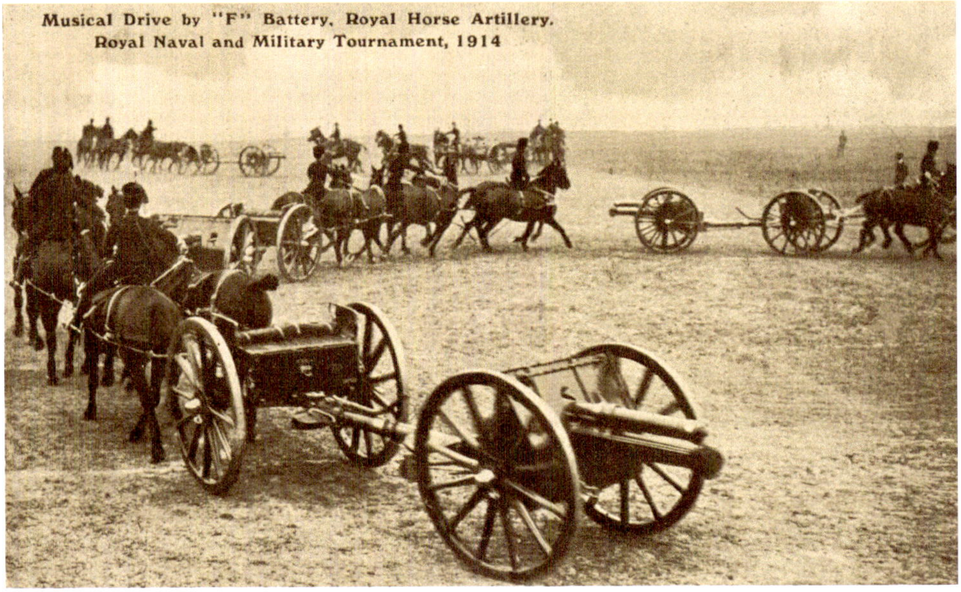


F Battery Royal Horse Artillery, naval and military tournament, *c.* 1914.

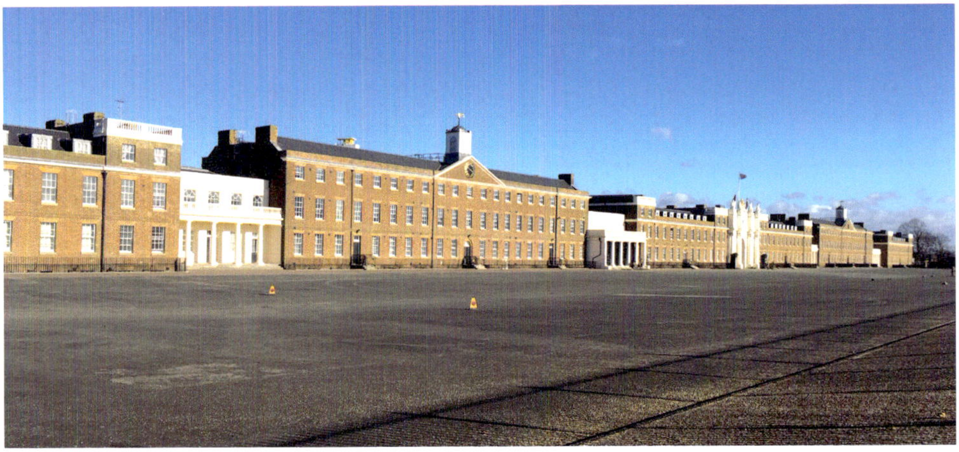

Royal Artillery Barracks before schedule closure in 2027.

Artillery. After almost 300 years based at Woolwich, the Royal Artillery relocated to Larkhill, Salisbury Plain, in July 2007.

The Royal Artillery was replaced by military personnel of the public duties line infantry battalion, along with the incremental companies of Foot Guards, followed by the Princess of Wales's Royal Regiment and later the 1st Battalion Royal Anglian Regiment. This was not the end of an artillery link to Woolwich, however, as in 2012, the King's Troop moved from St John's Woods Barracks to a new purpose-built barracks in Woolwich known as Napier Lines, off Repository Road.

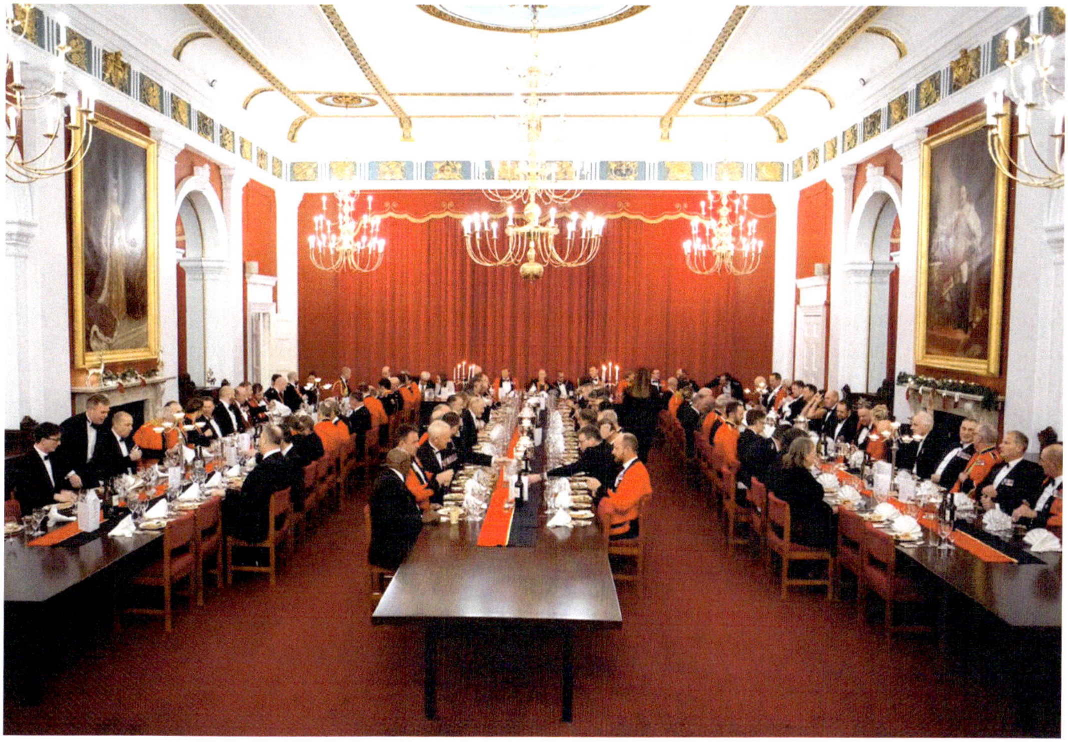

One of the last regimental dinners held at the Royal Artillery Barracks, *c.* 2024. (Courtesy of Woolwich Royal Artillery Barracks)

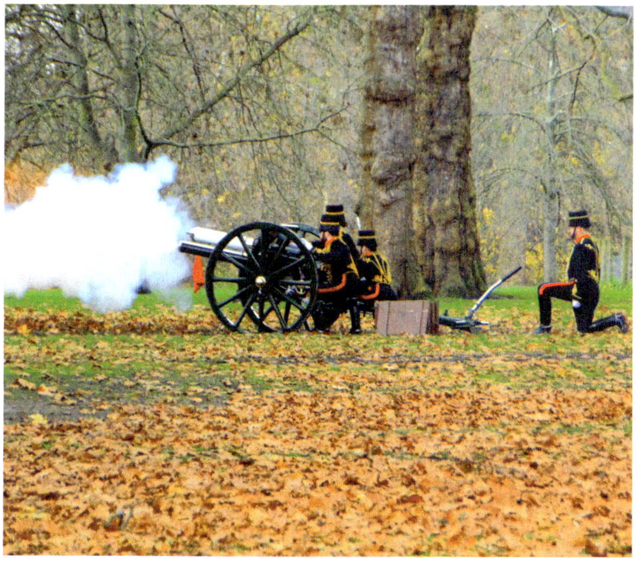

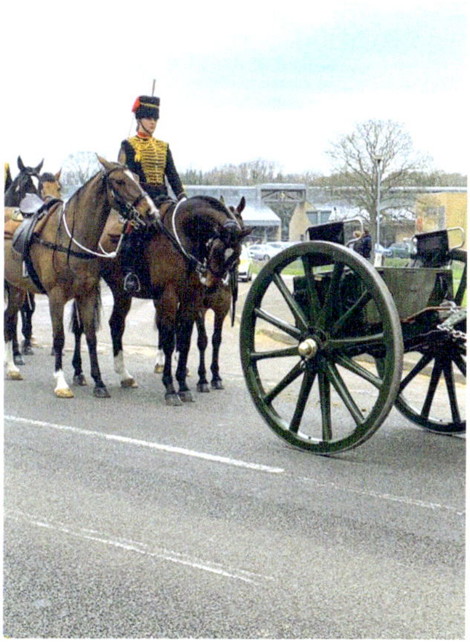

*Above left*: The King's Troop firing salute at Queen Elizabeth II's platinum jubilee, *c.* 2022.

*Above right*: King's Troop lead bombardier, Woolwich Napier Lines barracks.

The ceremonial unit was formed as a six-gun Royal Horse Artillery Battery following the Second World War after King George VI expressed his view that, as the Horse Artillery had become mechanised, a traditional troop of horse artillery should be retained to take part in ceremonial events. Known as the King's Troop, after Queen Elizabeth II's accession to the throne she declared the name would be made permanent to honour her father, the late king.

The King's Troop consists of approximately 140 members, of which almost half are now women, trained to care and drive the six teams, each team consisting of six horses in three pairs, each pair ridden by a trooper, bombardier at the front, a gunner in the centre and lance bombardier at the rear. Each team of six horses pull a carriage holding a First World War-era QF 13-pounder gun, which weighs around 1.5 tons.

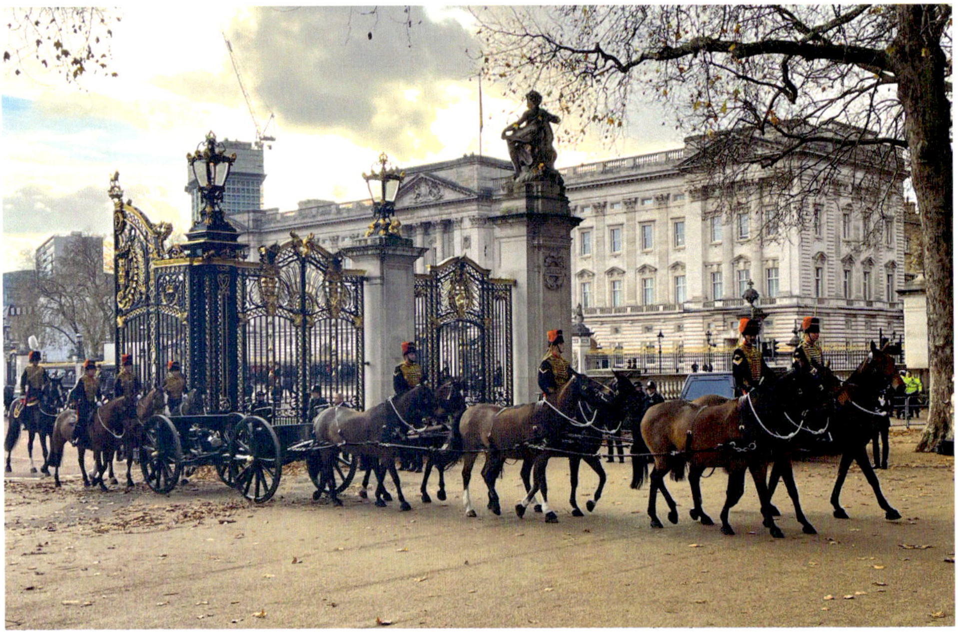

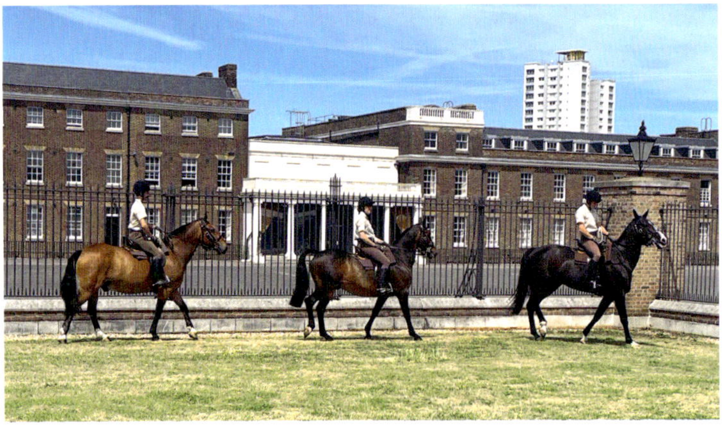

*Above*: King's Troop passing Buckingham Palace and entering Canada Gate, Green Park.

*Left*: King's Troop horses exercising, Woolwich Royal Artillery Barracks, c. 2025.

Each of the team members, dressed in traditional uniforms of black with red and gold brocade with variants for different state occasions, are not only excellent riders, they are also gunnery experts. King's Troop duties include firing royal salutes at the reigning monarch's birthday parade, the Lord Mayor's Show, state and military funerals, and, for one month each year, performing duties of the King's Life Guard at Horse Guards Parade.

In response to the threat of the Napoleonic Wars, the Woolwich division of the Royal Marines was formed in 1805 and housed in barracks on Frances Street, to the south of the Royal Dockyard. Providing a military presence in the dockyard, the Royal Marine Artillery, manning ships' guns, wore the blue uniform of the Royal Regiment of Artillery, while the Royal Marine infantry wore the red of the British infantry. The key role of the marines included engaging in musket fire on the enemy from British ships, fighting in boarding actions, ensuring the security of navy officers, and maintaining discipline among ship crews. The Woolwich division of Royal Marines was the shortest lived of the four Royal Marine divisions, disbanded in 1869 at the closure of the docks.

The 20th Battalion, London Regiment Blackheath and Woolwich, formed in 1908, was a unit of the Territorial Army, with its headquarters and garrison situated at Holly Hedge House, Blackheath, acquired for military use in 1887. The infantry regiment consisted of several small Rifle Volunteer Corps, dating back to 1859. The units, known as the Queen's Own Royal West Kent, were once situated at various locations throughout west Kent.

The regiment saw action during the First World War on the Western Front, in Palestine, and Salonica. The unit transformed into the 34th Anti-Aircraft Battalion and served as a searchlight battery during the Second World War. Deployed to defend the Thames Estuary and riverside industries in support of the anti-aircraft guns targeting German bombers during raids.

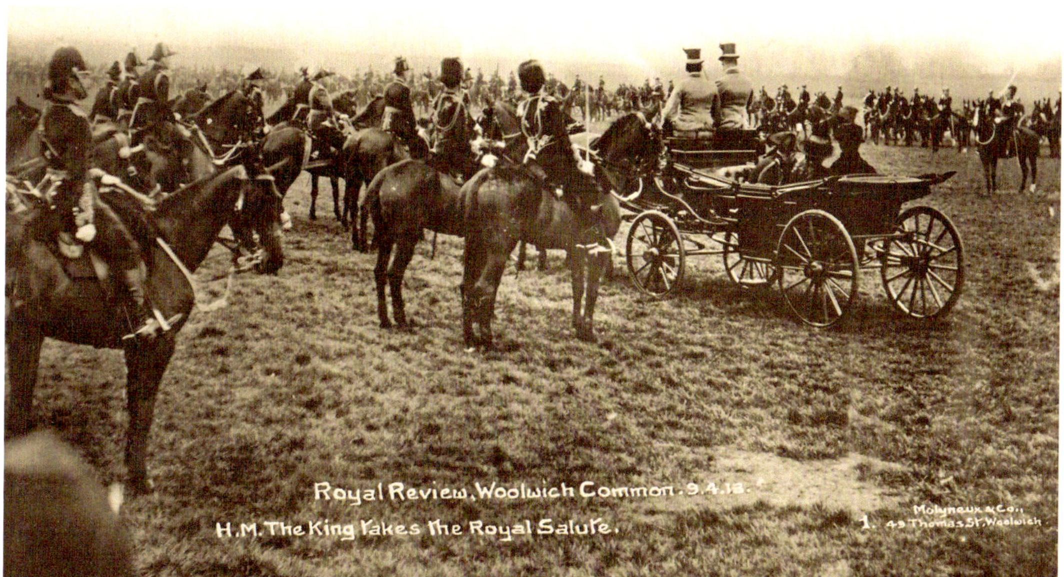


George V, Woolwich Common Royal Review, *c.* 1913.

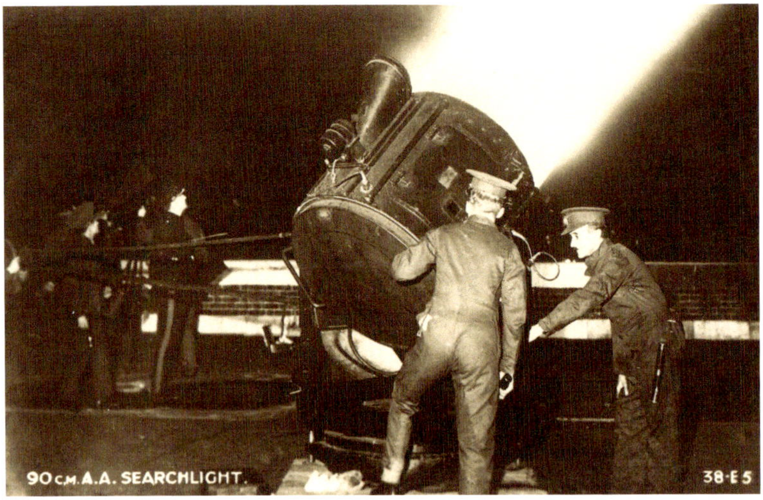


Anti-Aircraft Projector (searchlight) for illuminating enemy aircraft for anti-aircraft guns.

The original regimental house was irreparably damaged during a bombing raid and subsequently demolished. The existing drill hall was enlarged in 1946 to accommodate the battery, which had increased in size. Although the searchlight unit moved out in 1955, the drill hall was occupied by the 10th Battalion, the Parachute Regiment Rifle Company and is now a reserve centre for the C (London) Company of the 5th Battalion Royal Fusiliers, alongside the 94 Cadet Detachment Royal Regiment of Fusiliers.

A further defence against the Second World War bombing raids were barrage balloons raised above Blackheath, the balloons filled with hydrogen and tethered to the ground by steel cable. The balloons created obstacles for German aircraft, forcing them to fly higher and making the aircraft less effective in dropping bombs. The Blackheath barrage balloons were deployed by No. 1 Balloon Centre and 901 Squadron (a barrage balloon squadron of the Auxiliary Air Force) and No. 2 Installation Unit based at RAF Station Kidbrooke. Formed in 1937, Balloon Barrage Group No. 30, based at the Kidbrooke site, was the first balloon squadron. A squadron typically consisting of five balloons under the control of Fighter Command. Each barrage balloon was flown by two corporals and ten airmen. Later in the war, WAAF personnel operated the balloons to release men for active service.

RAF Kidbrooke was mainly in use as a support site, comprising up to 2,000 personnel, their roles included vehicle maintenance, ordnance repair, aircraft storage, and modification, along with balloon manufacture and repair. After the war, the base housed an RAF cargo-handling training centre, motor transport squadron, and linguistics school. Although some RAF storage buildings remain, the site has been transformed into a mixed-use of residential buildings, a school and National Maritime Museum storage facility.

The unofficial first company of women in the army was established at Woolwich in August 1914, the women volunteering to work in the Army Pay Service, a necessity through the expansion of a Regular and Regular Reserve Army from a peacetime strength of 200,000 in August 1914 to nearly 1 million by November 1914.

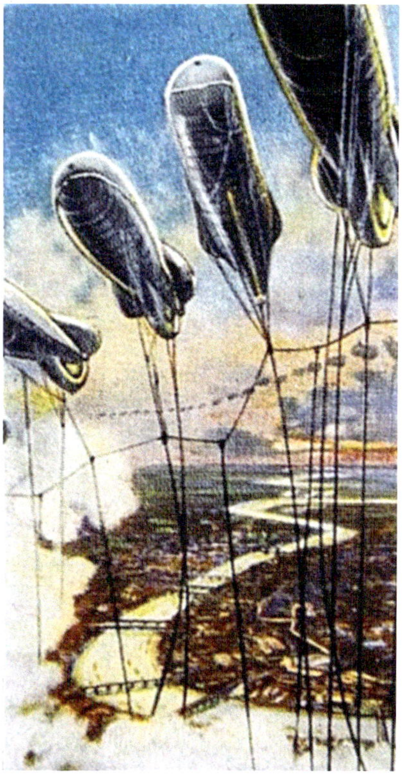

*Right*: Barrage balloons above London during the Second World War.

*Below*: Army Pay Office staff, Woolwich, *c.* 1920. (Courtesy of Dr John Black)

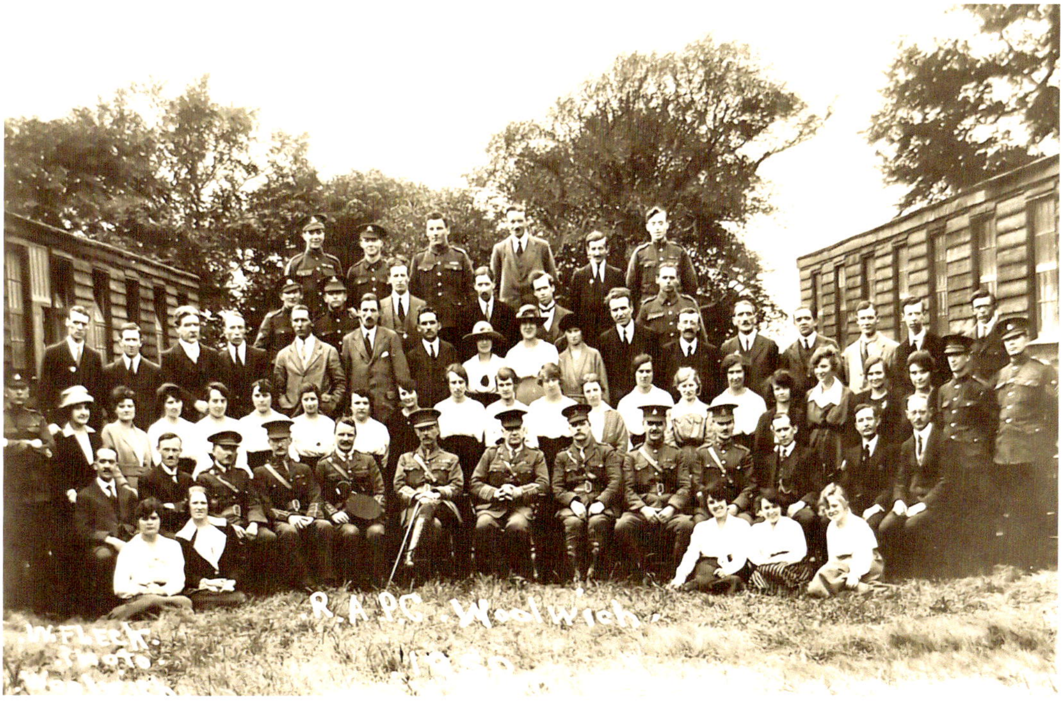

The placement of women volunteers at the Army Pay Office, Woolwich, was conducted unofficially, without any mandate from the War Office. In times past, it had been customary for the wives of military officers to assist and support the families of soldiers during times of war, activities which came to prominence during and after the Crimean War, and the women Army Pay Office volunteers at Woolwich were a continuation of regimental patronage traditions.

The military within the borough has long associations with nursing, dating back to the Crimean War when Florence Nightingale was influential in the care of injured soldiers and the development of an official scheme for military hospital female nursing.

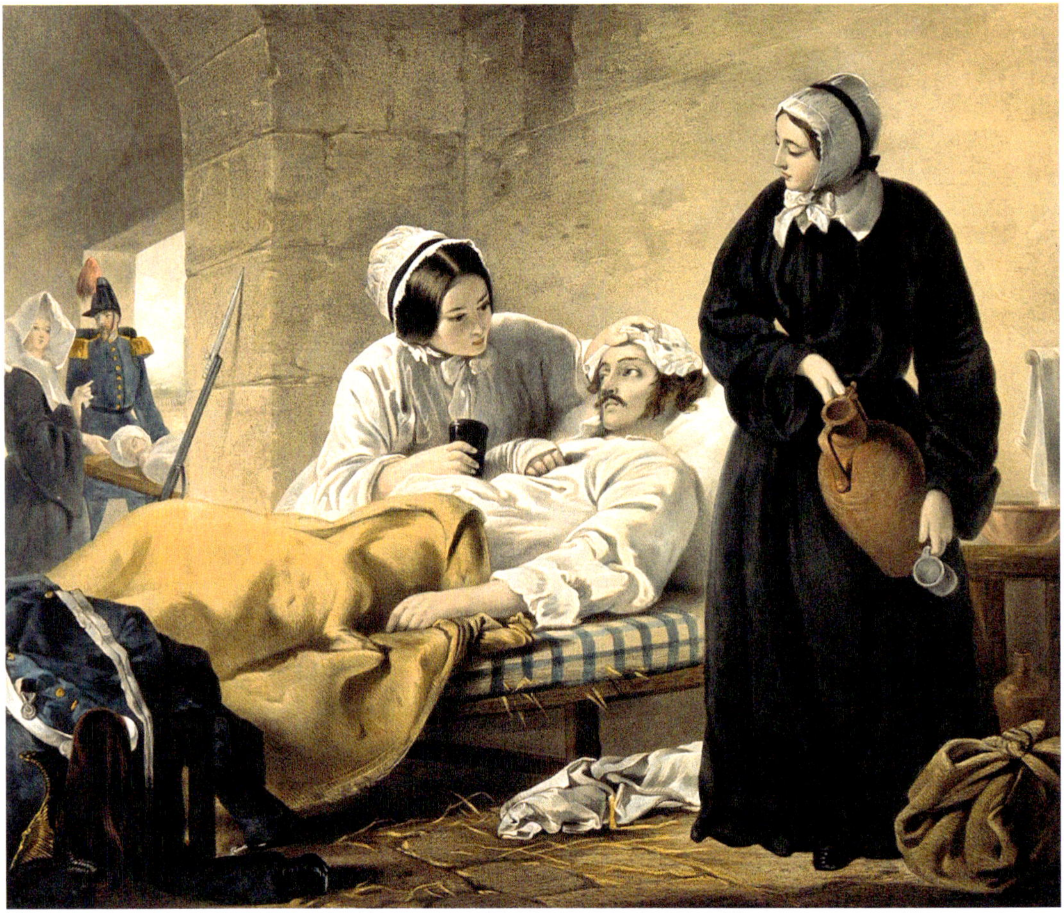

British troops being cared for at Crimea by Nightingale's nurses, many of whom were self-funded volunteers. (Courtesy of the Wellcome Collection)

# 5. Military Buildings

Situated on the Southbank of the Thames, the most recognised military building located in Greenwich is the former Royal Hospital, established in 1692.

By the mid-nineteenth century, it became financially prudent for hospital residents to receive allowances as out-pensioners, almost 1,000 of 1,400 pensioners electing to leave before the hospital finally closed in 1869.

Designed by architects Sir Christopher Wren and Nicholas Hawksmoor, finance came through public fundraising, Treasury contributions and pirates' confiscated booty.

After acquired by the Royal Navy, the palatial buildings were used as a college for the education of Royal Navy officers, consisting of classrooms, lecture theatres, and residential accommodation. During the Second World War, approximately 27,000 naval officers and 8,000 WRNS trained at the college. After the war, naval officers from all parts of the globe came to study navigation, sciences, mathematics, and the administrative staffing polices of their profession.

Two of Britain's recent royals studied at the naval college: Prince Philip, Duke of Edinburgh, attended in 1948, two years after becoming Baron of Greenwich, followed by his eldest son, Prince Charles, in 1975.

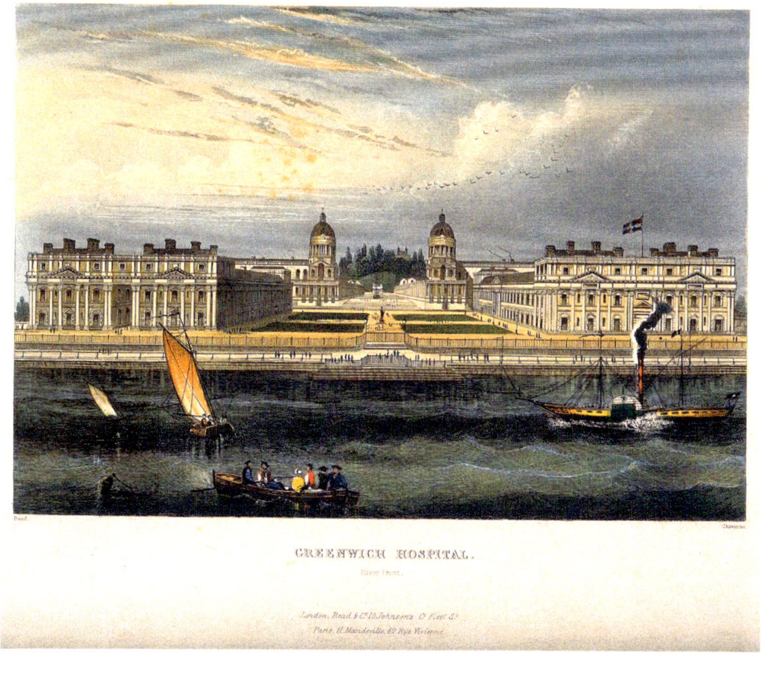


Greenwich Hospital, later the Royal Naval College, *c.* 1800.

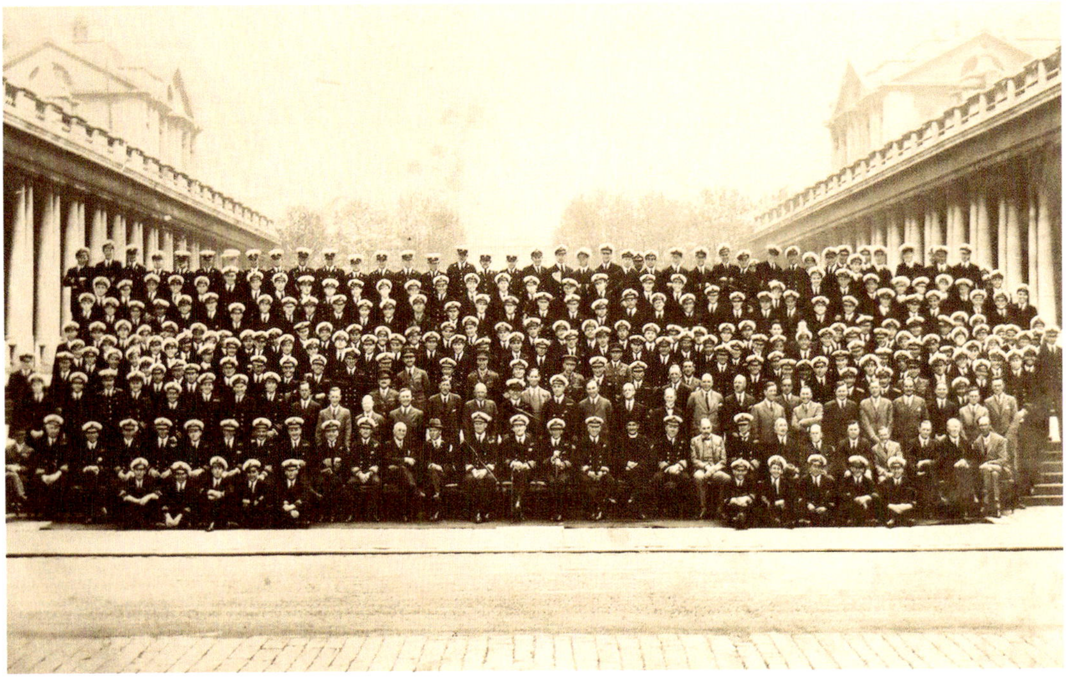

Royal Naval College officer students and staff, *c.* 1900.

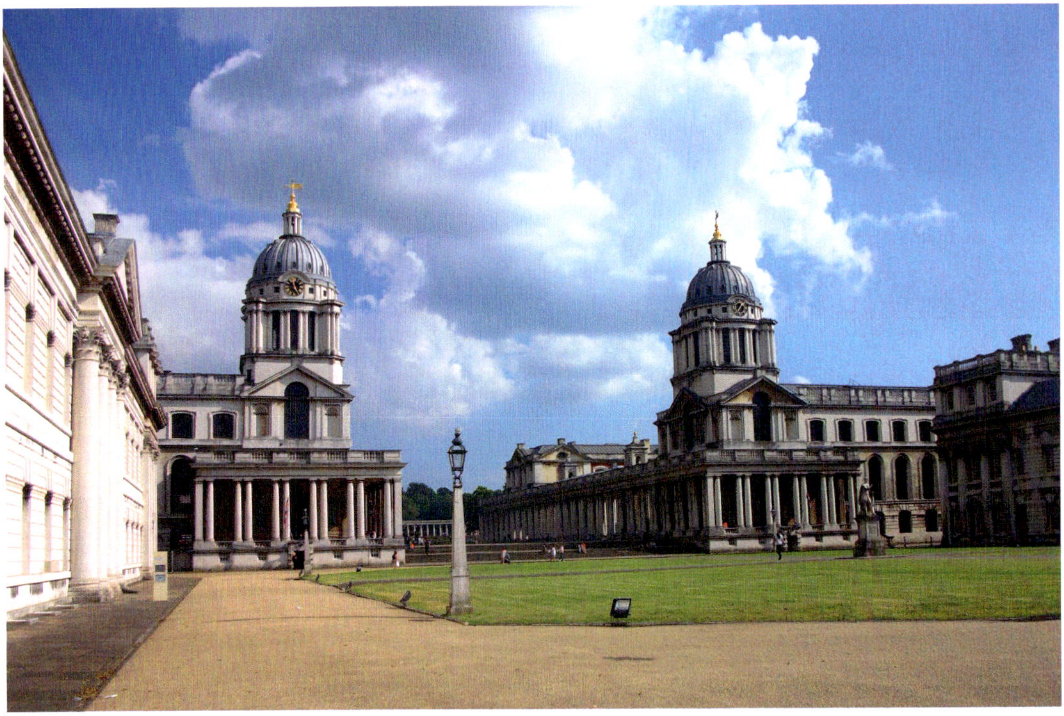

Royal Naval College: Queen Mary Quarter (left) and King William Quarter (right).

In 1959, the Naval Department of Nuclear Science and Technology installed Jason, a nuclear reactor, in the King William Quarter, one of the few reactors in the United Kingdom operating in a highly populated area. Warships of various sizes often moored off the Royal Naval College, and although no longer a naval base, naval vessels can occasionally still be seen close to Greenwich Pier. After the navy moved out in 1998, the buildings became home to Greenwich University and Trinity Laban Conservatoire of Music and Dance.

Opposite the Old Royal Naval College are the buildings of the former Royal Hospital School, now the National Maritime Museum, where orphaned boys, along with sons of seafarers killed in service, were boarded and educated under the care of Greenwich Pensioners. Established in 1758, King George III granted the Queen's House to be used as a small school, originally located near King William Walk.

Over the years, the hospital school buildings were enlarged with new wings added for dormitories, classrooms, and dining areas. By the late 1800s, the school was caring for

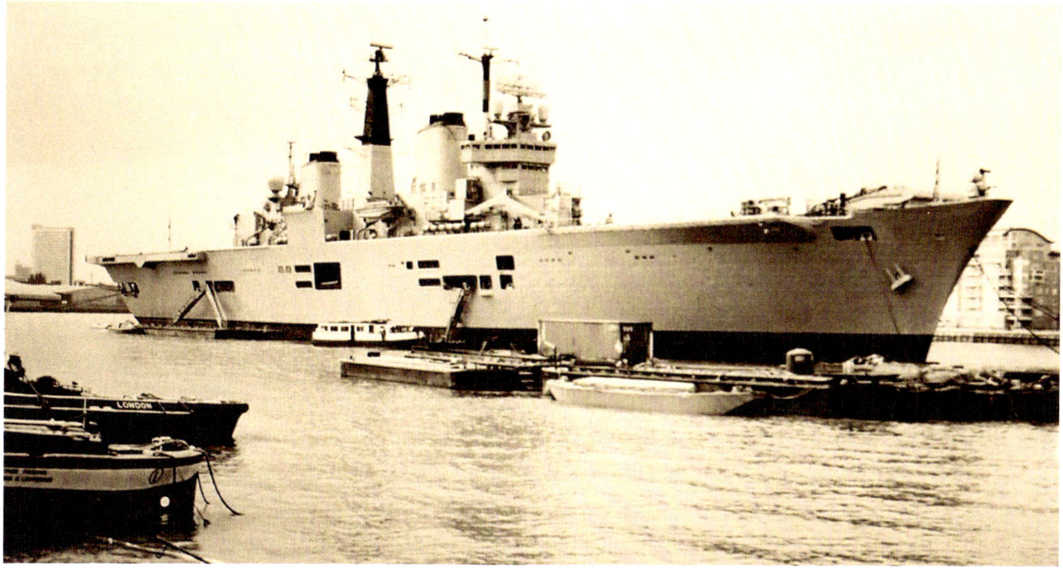

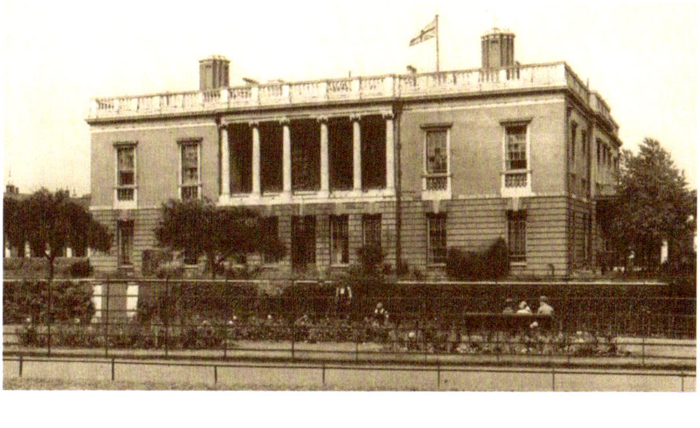

*Above*: Falklands veteran HMS *Invincible* at Greenwich in July 2005, which played a leading role in the Trafalgar Bicentenary. (Courtesy of A. Phinbow)

*Right*: The Queen's House, built between 1616 and 1635.

over 1,000 boys, where between 1874 and 1930, 10,000 had joined the navy, five going on to become admirals.

Although it was customary practice for boy sailors to learn the art of firing cannons and repelling boarders, warfare had moved on, and the latest advances in navigation and gunnery were also an integral part of their education.

At one time, young girls attended the school for education in domestic services. By the early 1930s, the school was oversubscribed and relocated to a larger site at Holbrook, Suffolk, with the Greenwich buildings acquired by the National Maritime Museum.

Across the small tidal river known as Deptford Creek was the site of Royal Deptford Dockyard.

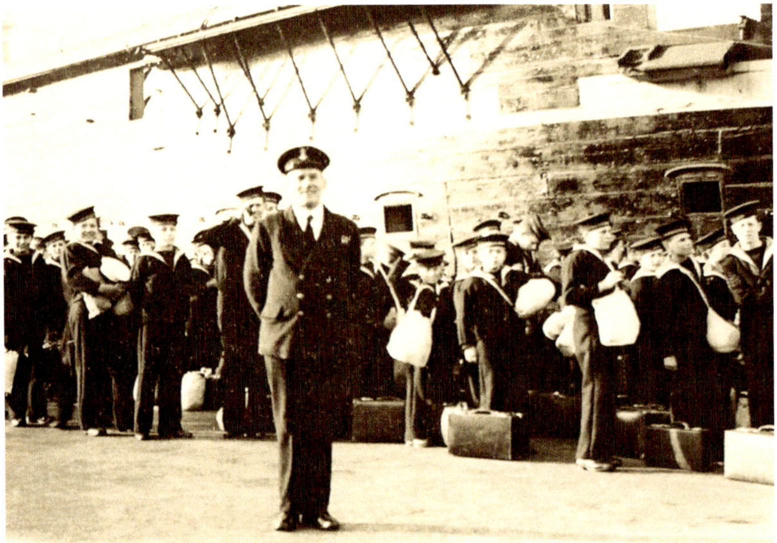

Mr Bushell Hospital School staff member with trainee boy sailors and static training ship *Fame*, c. 1923.

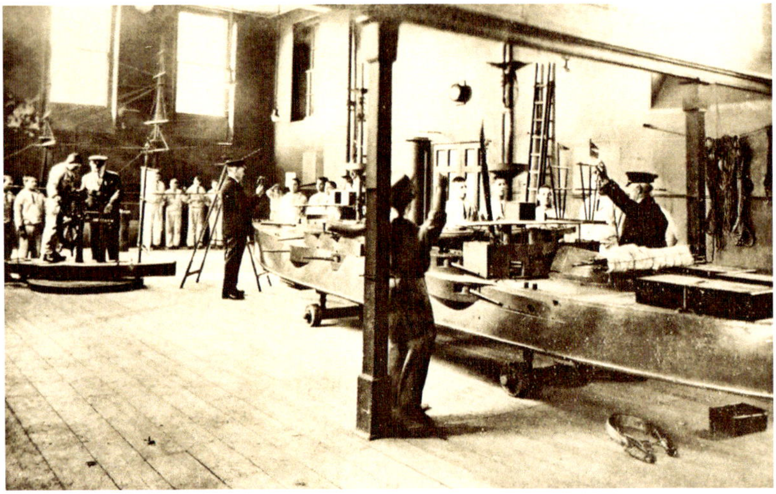

Seamanship Room Hospital School, c. 1928.

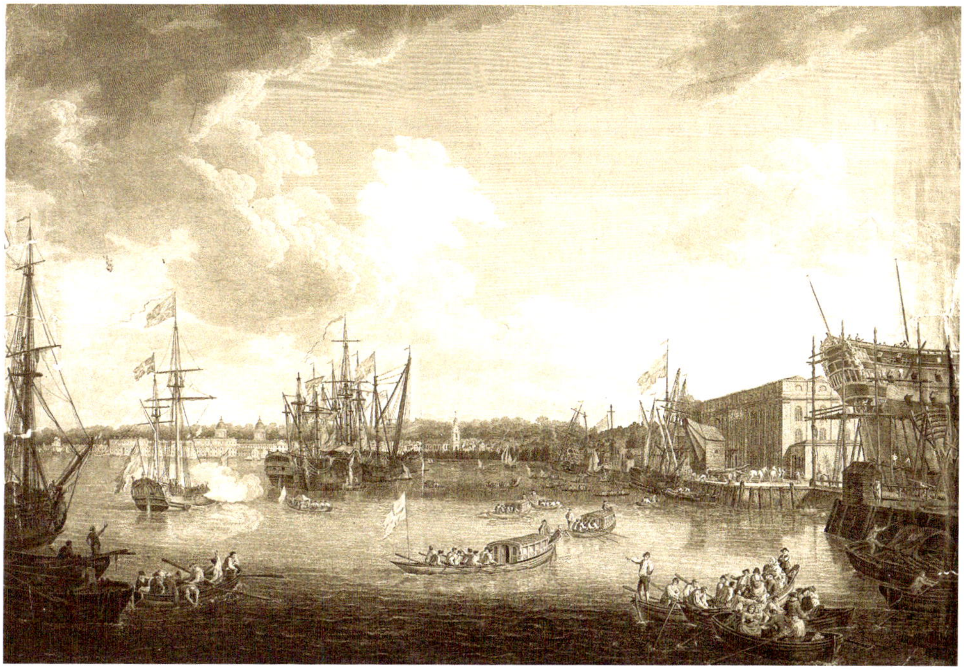

Royal Dockyard, Deptford, late 1700s.

Very few buildings remain from a time when naval warships were built and launched. Those that survive are later dockyard additions and include entrance gates to the Royal Victoria Victualing Yards, the Georgian-built former dockyard storehouses, administration offices and Master Shipwright's House, and a set of riverside gates and steps.

Although many dockyard buildings were damaged during Second World War bombing raids, those that survived until the late 1950s were subsequently demolished and the slips and dock basins filled in to make way for a large social housing project, Pepys Estate, named

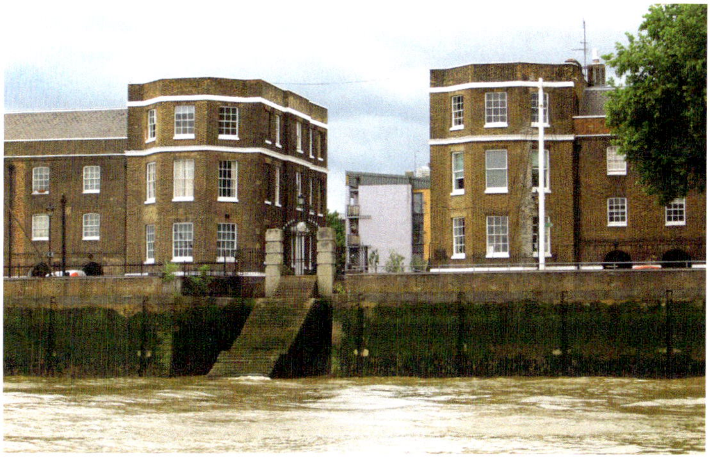

The late eighteenth-century Deptford Dockyard victualling buildings survived redevelopment in the 1970s.

after Royal Naval Administrator Samuel Pepys. Adjacent to Pepys Estate, an area of land retained by the navy, which served as Royal Naval Store Depot, was sold off in the 1980s.

Used mostly for storage, the site Convoys Wharf is currently awaiting redevelopment, although the Grade II listed Olympia Shed storehouse survives.

To the east of the Meridian Line, running through the centre of Greenwich, Vanbrugh Castle is situated towards the top of Maze Hill, opposite Greenwich Park. Erected between 1717 and 1719, designed as a private dwelling by architect, playwright and one-time English spy Sir John Vanbrugh, the castle was modelled along the lines of the Bastille in France, where Vanbrugh was imprisoned for spying in 1690.

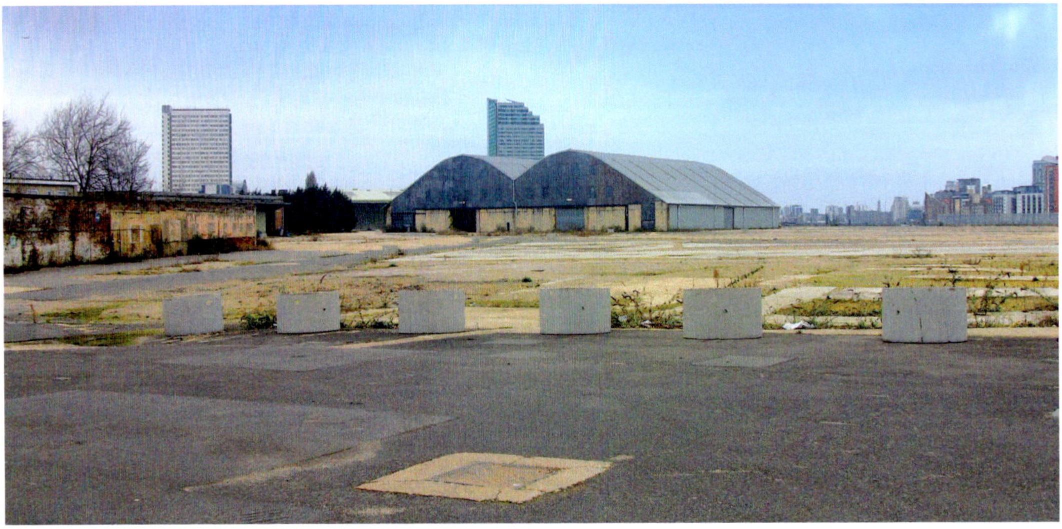

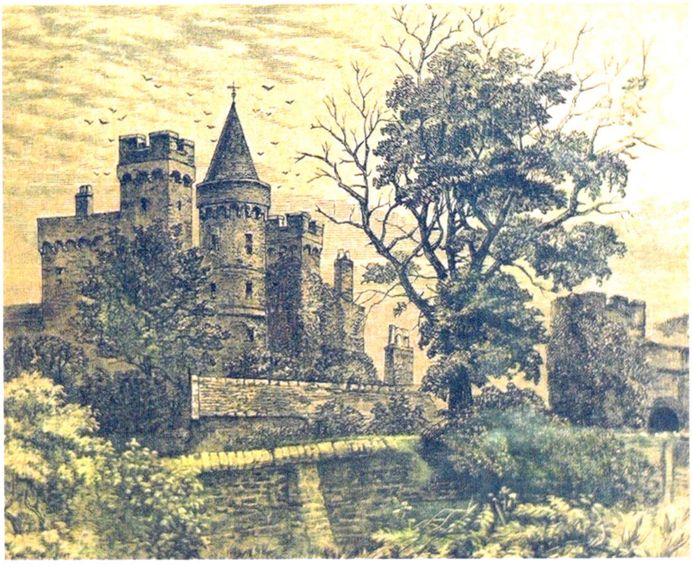

*Above*: Olympic Shed, Convoys Wharf, awaiting redevelopment in the early 2000s.

*Left*: Vanbrugh Castle, Maze Hill, was built during the early 1700s.

Vanbrugh added to the castellated medieval-style fortification before he died in 1726, and further additions and alterations were made by a succession of owners before the castle was donated to the RAF Benevolent Fund in 1920 by owner Blackheath-born oil merchant Alexander Duckham.

The castle was converted into a school for the children of RAF personnel killed in service. The students were evacuated to Sussex during the Second World War until the end of hostilities. It was well known by students that there were secret tunnels below the castle, one exiting in woods known as the Dell, and a large underground room they named the Dungeon, came in use as a secret smoking den. When the school relocated in 1975, the Grade II listed castle returned to private ownership.

Overlooking the Thames from a plateau at the centre of Greenwich Park is the Old Royal Observatory. Commissioned by Charles II in 1675, the observatory was established primarily to perfect the art of accurate astronomical navigation at sea for the benefit of the king's naval ships, as well as vessels trading around the globe to enrich both crown and country.

The king donated £500 and reclaimed material from a demolished Tower of London gatehouse and unused bricks from Tilbury Fort for the building's construction, erected on the fifteenth-century Greenwich Castle site. On top of Flamsteed House, the observatory's main building, named after the first Astronomer Royal, John Flamsteed, a bright red ball was installed on the west tower used as an aid to shipping on the Thames. The ball rises

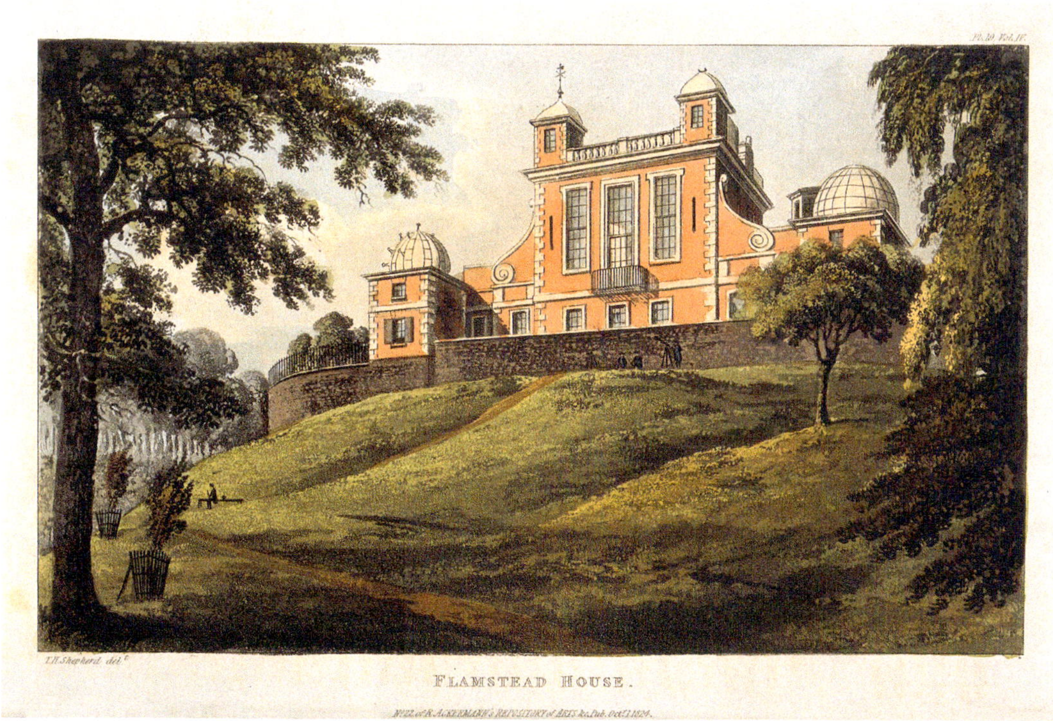


Flamsteed House, principle building of Greenwich Royal Observatory, was established in 1674.

to the top of the mast at 12.58 p.m. and drops at exactly 1 p.m., a signal to ship navigators for setting their time pieces.

After the Royal Observatory relocated to Herstmonceux, Sussex, in 1957 due to the light pollution in London, the Greenwich buildings were opened as a museum of astronomy, navigation and timekeeping.

Adjacent to the observatory is the statue dedicated to James Wolfe, victor of Quebec, whose parents resided at Macartney House, a large seventeenth-century building situated on the boundary wall at the south-west corner of the park.

Since first built, the Grade II listed Macartney House has been added to throughout the following centuries and has now been converted into apartments.

A much larger and grander private residence, Charlton House, a Jacobean manor built on instruction by the crown to house Sir Adam Newton, tutor of James I's son, Prince Charles, was utilised towards the end of the First World War as a hospital for wounded service personnel.

One-time home of British Army officer and politician Sir Thomas Spencer Wilson, whose son-in-law Spencer Percival served as prime minister until assassinated in May 1812, Charlton House was loaned by the Spencer-Wilson family for use as the headquarters of the Red Cross affiliated to the Brook War Hospital, staffed by members of the Voluntary Aid detachments from the Greenwich and Woolwich divisions. Sold to

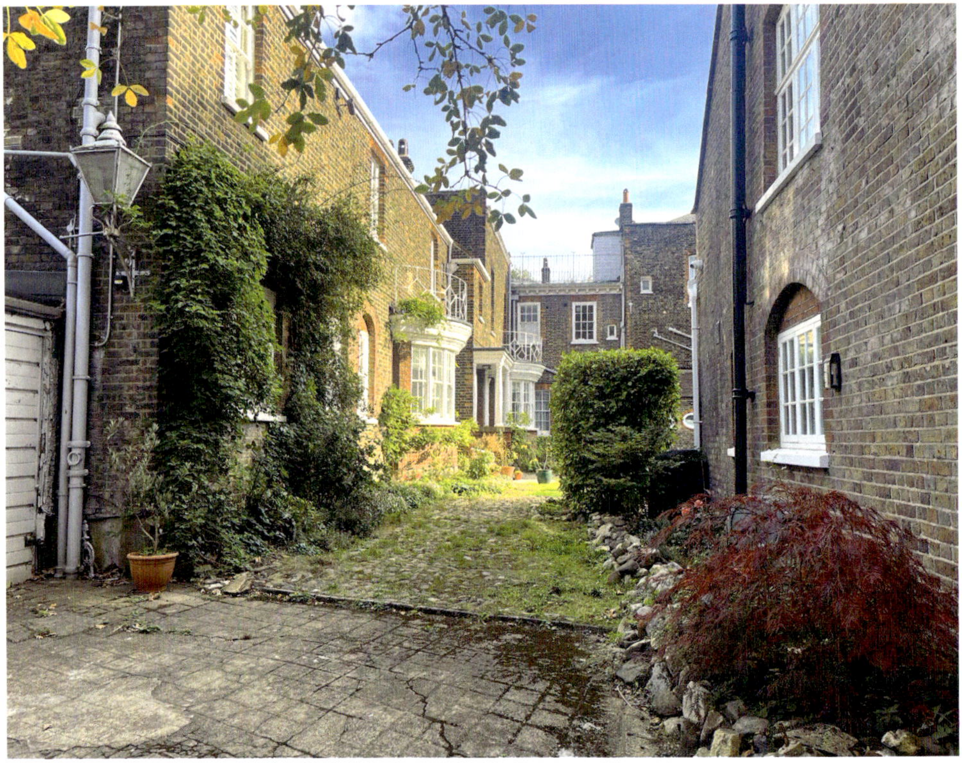

Wolfe family residence, Macartney House, Chesterfield Walk, erected late 1600s.

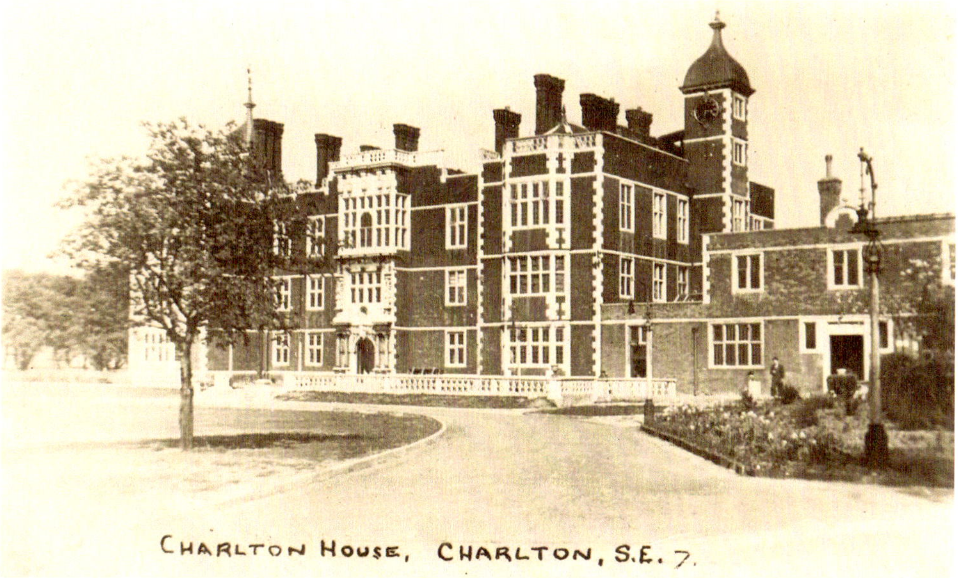


Jacobean-built Charlton House, Charlton village.

the Metropolitan Borough of Greenwich in 1925, Charlton House is now a community centre run by the Royal Greenwich Heritage Trust.

Originally built as a fever hospital in the late 1800s, the Brook War Hospital was requisitioned by the War Office at the outbreak of the Second World War, one of three military hospitals situated on Shooters Hill.

Closed in 1996, a majority of Brook General Hospital buildings were demolished to make way for housing, with only the water tower, entrance lodge, administration block,

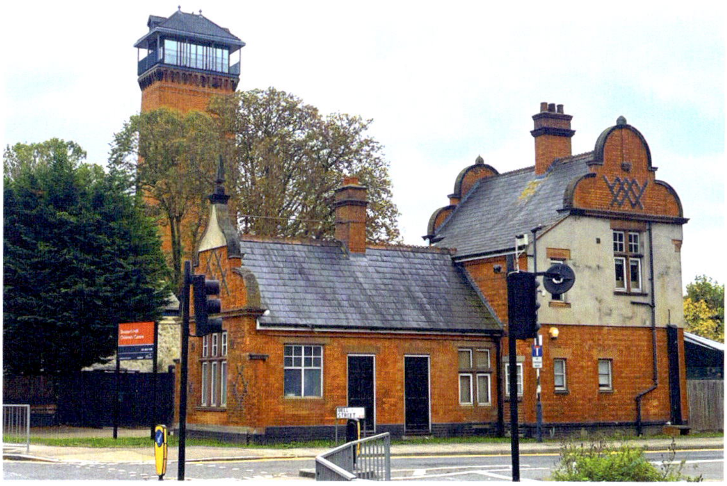

Former Brook Hospital's main entrance.

and steward's house retained. The other two military hospitals, the Royal Herbert and the Memorial, survived. The oldest, the Royal Herbert Hospital, was built as a restorative facility for British veterans of the Crimea War under the direction of Sidney Herbert, former Secretary of War, the hospital opening in 1865. Designed by architect Sir Douglas Galton of the Royal Engineers with input from Florence Nightingale, his cousin by marriage, the layout was based on a pavilion style favoured by Nightingale, with each ward connected to a central corridor, maximising daylight and fresh air. This design and patient treatment paved the way forward for future military and public hospitals. After Queen Victoria visited Boer War injured soldiers there in 1900, the hospital attained royal patronage.

Caring for wounded service personnel during both the First and Second World Wars, the hospital admitted civilian patients from the Royal Arsenal site after being bombed by the Luftwaffe, as well as caring for injured German aircrew downed during raids.

The hospital became the army's orthopaedic centre and medical training centre until closure in 1977, when the Grade II listed buildings were transformed into exclusive apartments, renamed the Royal Herbert Pavilions.

The Memorial Hospital was established after the First World War as a lasting memorial to the war dead from the local area, and a replacement for both Woolwich and Plumstead Cottage hospitals. Opened in 1927 by the Duke and Duchess of York, later King George VI and Queen Elizabeth, the hospital became a military facility during the Second World War, providing support for the Royal Herbert Hospital.

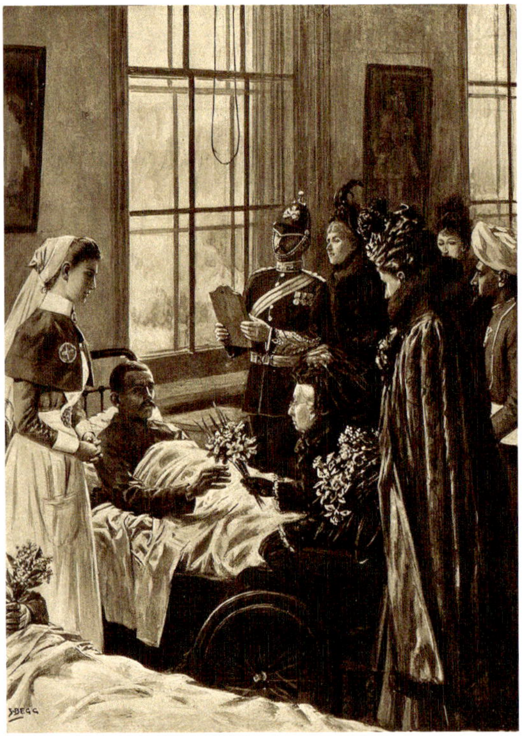

Queen Victoria visits a Boer War patient at Herbert Hospital in March 1822.

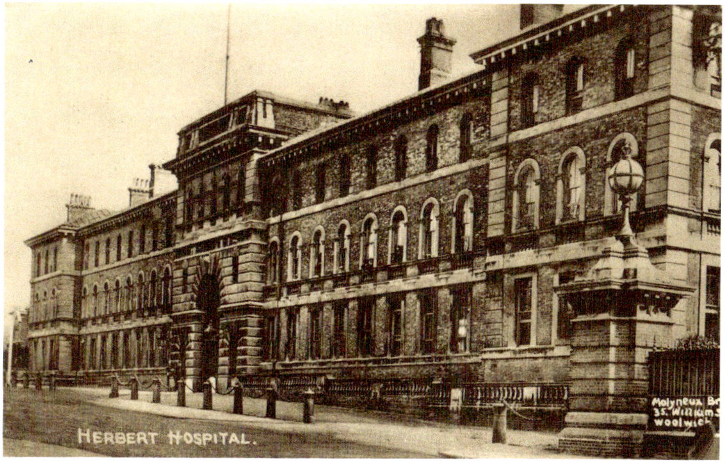


*Right*: Royal Herbert Hospital, opened 1866.

*Below*: The Memorial Hospital, Shooters Hill, opened in 1927.

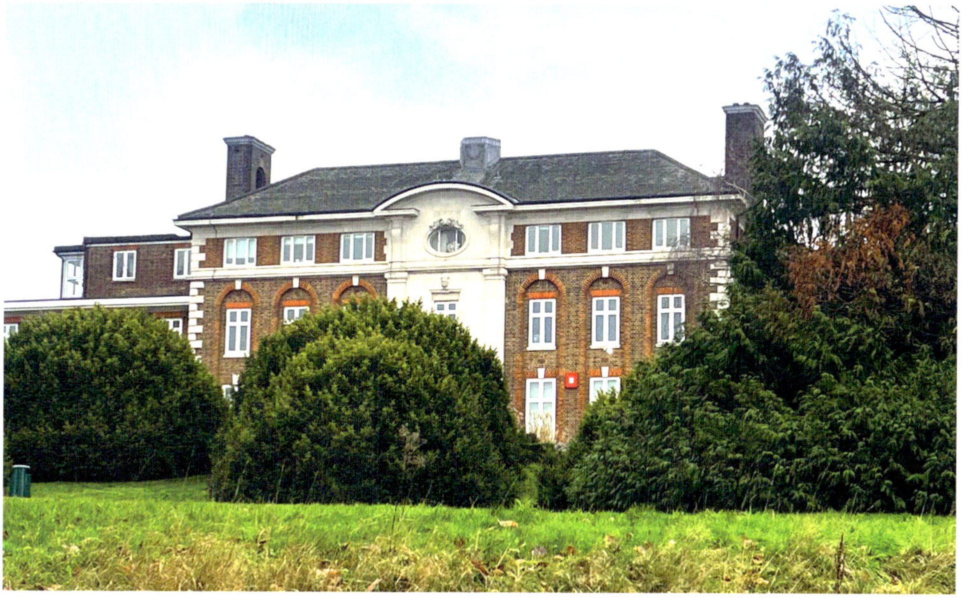

Specialising in surgery during the late 1960s, after inclusion into the National Health Service as a general hospital in the 1970s, the Memorial Hospital now serves as a day centre for the elderly and facility for psychiatric patients. Held in trust as a war memorial, the hospital cannot be sold for redevelopment.

Leading off from Shooters Hill, Academy Road runs northwards to Woolwich, where on the eastern side are the Tudor Gothic-style academy buildings from which the road takes its name.

The Royal Military Academy was founded for training officers and artillery engineers located at the Warren within the armaments site, gaining royal status in 1760. Outgrowing the building known as 'the Shop', a converted armaments workshop, the academy

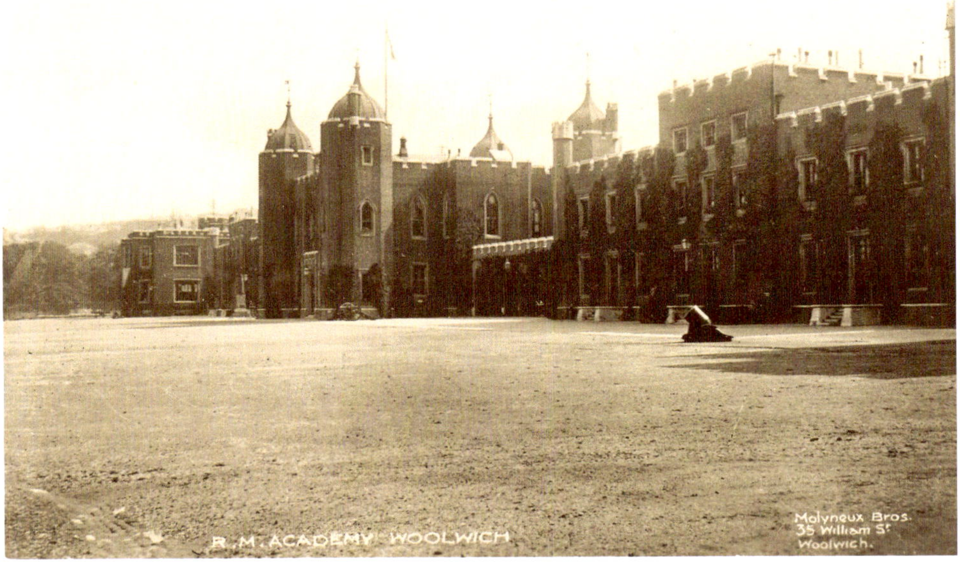


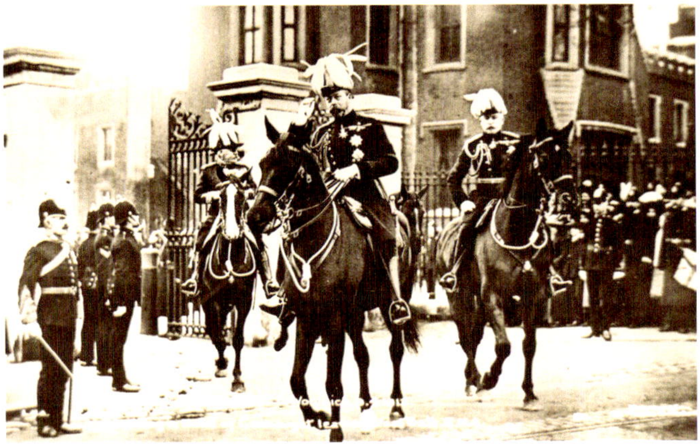

*Above*: Tudor Gothic-style Royal Military Academy, erected 1796–1805.

*Left*: George IV leaving the academy after a visit in 1913.

relocated to the impressive buildings adjacent to Woolwich Common in the early 1800s. Designed by Board of Ordnance architect James Wyatt, the academy consisted of a central block and a pair of accommodation wings linked by arcaded walkways. Enlarged in the 1860s to increase the number of cadets attending, the original central block was rebuilt after a fire.

Following the Second World War, the academy became part of the Woolwich Garrison, the chapel replacing the bombed-out Garrison Church of St George. Surplus to requirements by the early 2000s, the academy closed and was sold for conversion into residential properties.

The Garrison Church of St George, off Grand Depot Road, replaced the early Garrison Church built as part of the Royal Artillery Barracks opposite. Designed by brothers Thomas and Matthew Wyatt, great-grandsons of Royal Academy and Royal Artillery

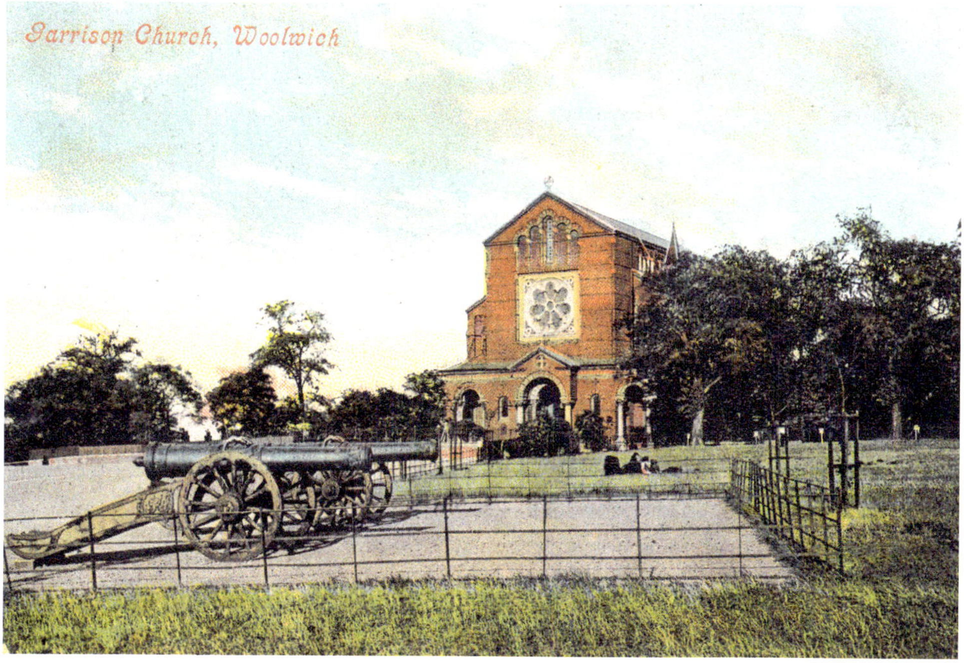


St George's Garrison Church, completed in 1863.

Barracks architect James Wyatt, the church was reminiscent of an early Lombardic Romanesque style.

After seating capacity was increased from 1,550 to 1,700, funds were raised by artillery officers to install two stained-glass windows and an organ. The interior was embellished with various decorative mosaics and memorials dedicated to artillery personnel who died in the Boer War.

The Garrison Church suffered considerable damage when struck by a V-1 flying bomb during the Second World War. Although a temporary roof was erected, it was no longer fit for purpose and fell into a poor state of repair.

After ownership transferred to Heritage of London Trust Operations, a Heritage Lottery Fund grant was awarded to assist with the costs for conservation work and the erection of a canopy roof. The restored ruin, under the direction of the Woolwich Garrison Church Trust, is now a public community space.

To the east of the church is a small secluded residential complex on Connaught Mews, one time site of the Royal Artillery Maternity Hospital, England's first military hospital. The existing building, erected in 1780, now known as Lantern House, was accompanied by two later buildings erected in 1801: Artillery House and Nightingale House. The site was then extended northwards, and when the Royal Herbert Hospital opened in 1865 the buildings were converted into barracks.

When the barracks were sold in the early 1960s, many of the buildings were demolished for redevelopment; however, the three main houses were converted into residential properties.

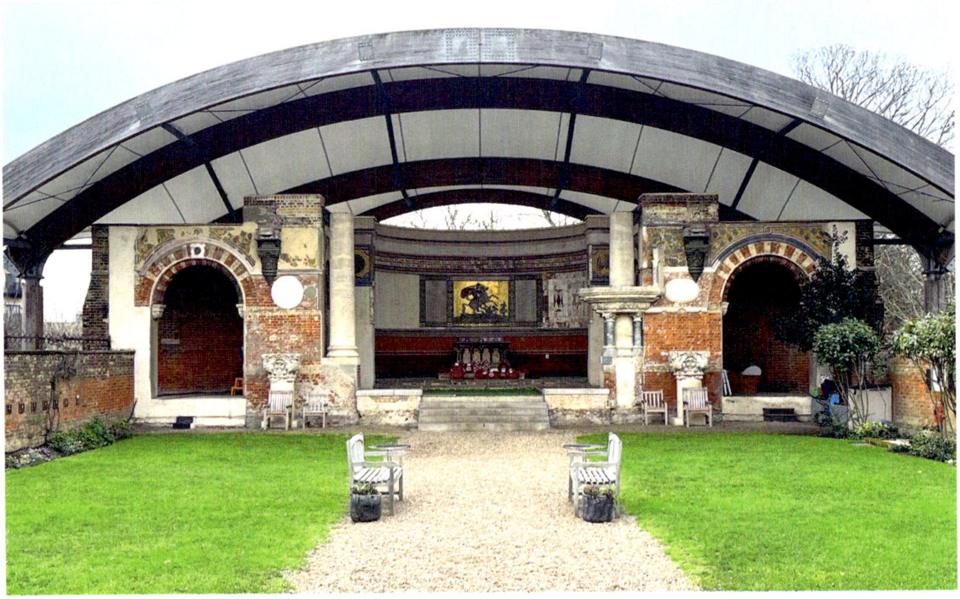

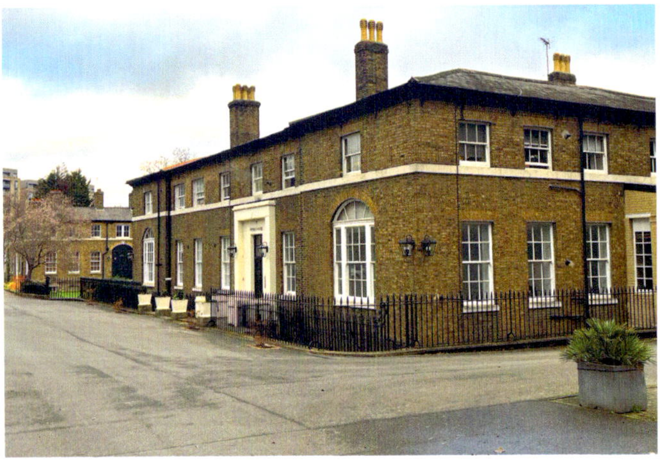

*Above*: Renovated apse and contemporary canopy covering for Garrison Church.

*Left*: Connaught Barracks renovated buildings, converted to residential apartments in the early 1990s.

Reputed to be the longest Georgian architectural façade in Europe, the Royal Artillery Barracks, situated adjacent to Artillery Place, housed up to 4,000 service personnel. Once the headquarters of the Royal Regiment of Artillery, the impressive building and parade ground were part of Woolwich Garrison. Originally quartered at the Warren, the regiment relocated to the newly built barracks in 1776. Laid out in a grid formation with internal roads, the soldiers' two accommodation blocks to the south were each flanked by officers' quarters. The complex included a chapel, library, officers mess, battalion and senior commanders' offices, guard house, prison cells, cook houses and canteen.

By the end of the 1700s the regiment had increased and architect James Wyatt was commissioned to conduct the works to enlarge the barracks. Following the Second World

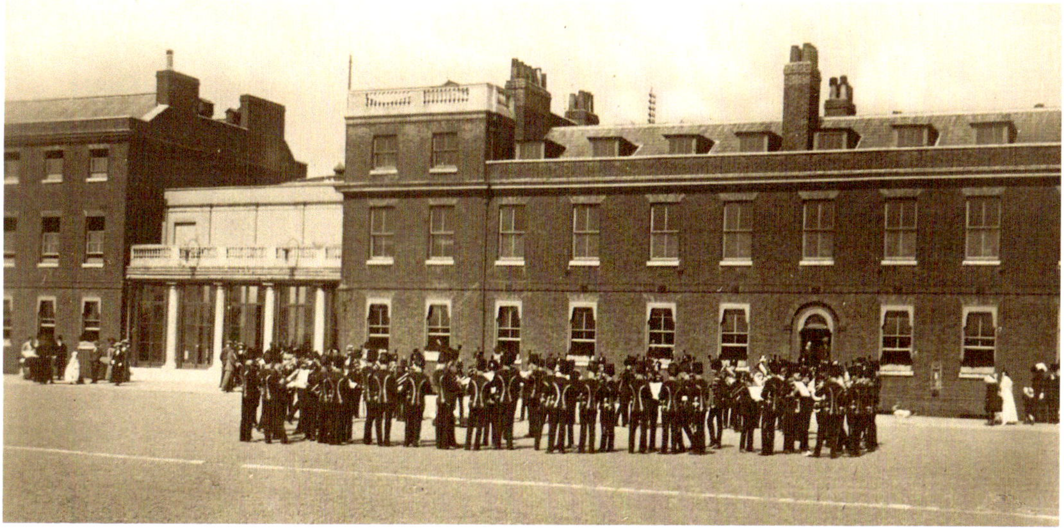

*Above*: Royal Artillery Band mustering in front of the Royal Artillery Barracks, early 1900s.

*Right*: Royal Artillery Barracks, reputed to be the longest Georgian façade in Europe at over 300 metres.

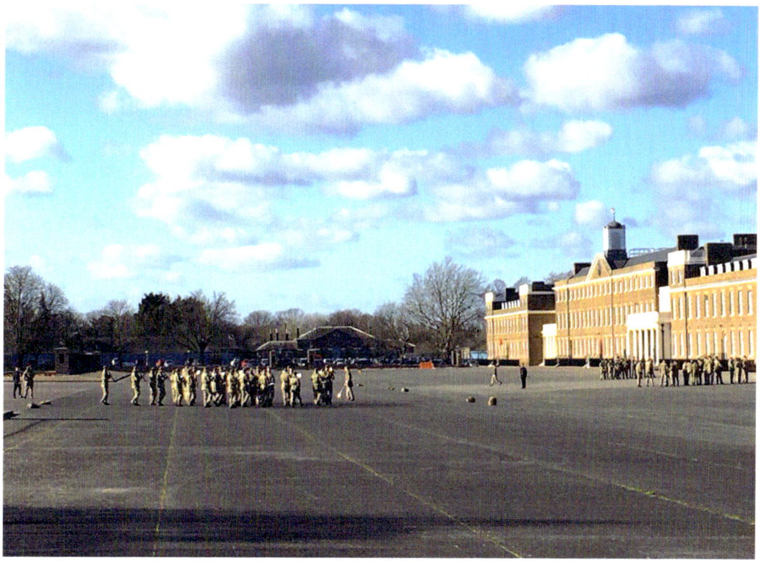

War, the barracks went through a rebuilding programme, with the long frontage to the south – Grade II listed in 1973 – retained. Although currently in operation as a barracks facility, the whole complex faced an uncertain future as the MOD decided to sell the site for residential and leisure development.

Off Repository Road to the north of Napier Lines, home to the King's Troop Royal Artillery, is a building known as the Rotunda, a circular-shaped brick building with a tent-shaped lead roof. The Rotunda was originally a twenty-four-sided polygon-shaped temporary structure relocated to Woolwich from Carlton House, a mansion in Westminster, in use at the time as a ballroom to celebrate the allied victory over Napoleon.

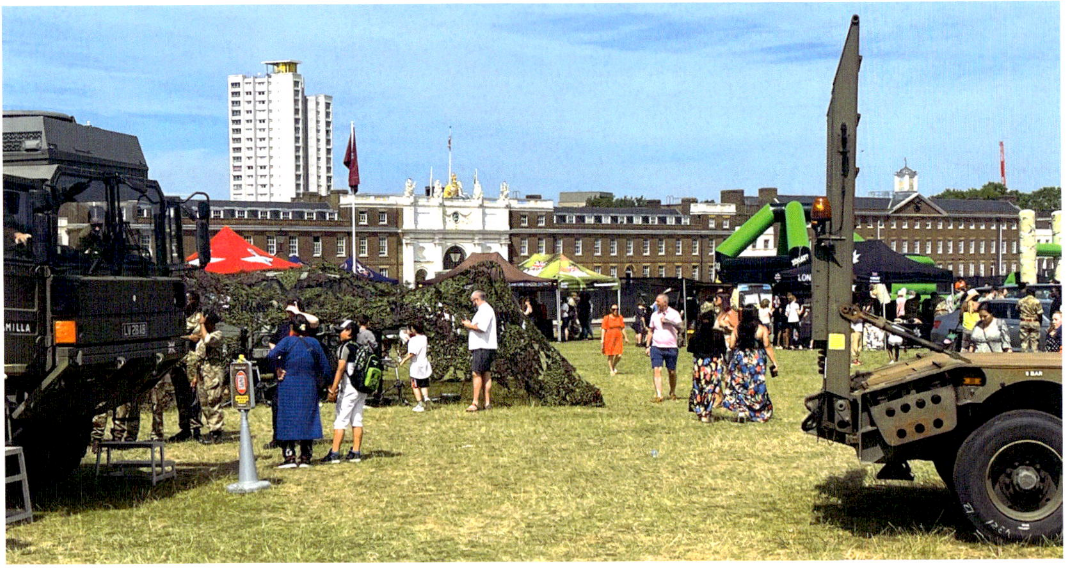

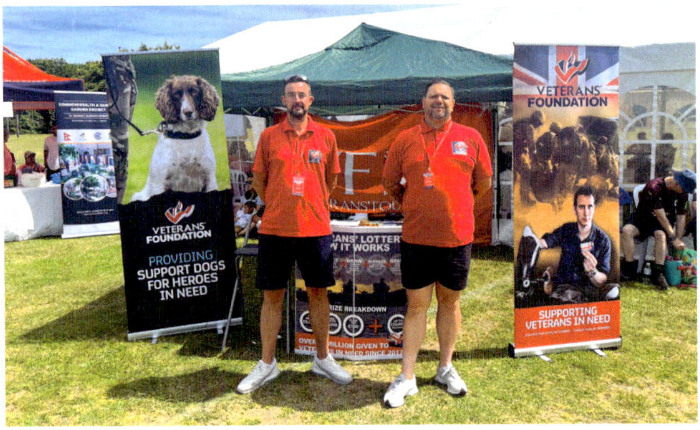


*Above*: Armed Forces Day, the Royal Artillery Barracks, summer 2025.

*Left*: Veterans Foundation fundraising, Armed Forces Day, 2025.

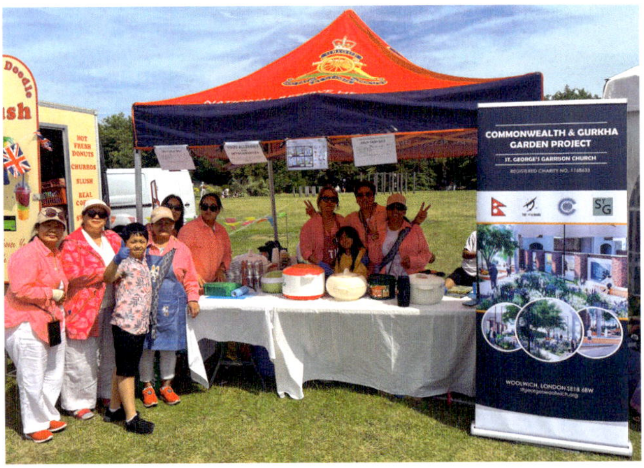


One of many community groups supporting Armed Forces Day, 2025.

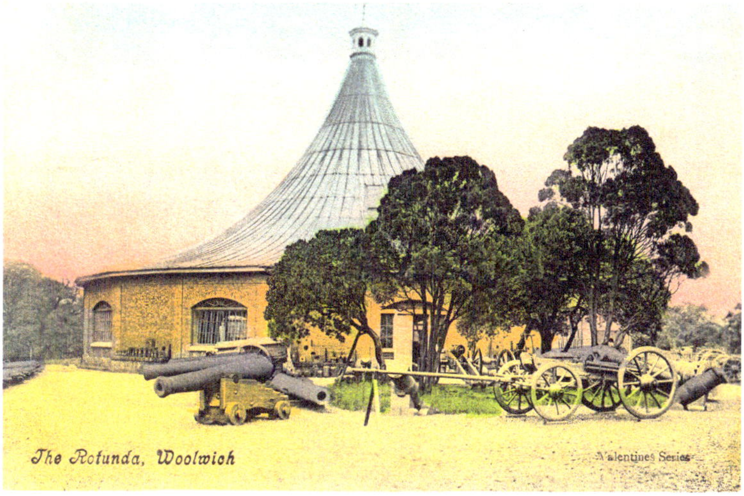


Rotunda Woolwich Common, used as a royal artillery museum until 1999.

After being re-erected, the Rotunda underwent modification to make it a permanent structure used as the Royal Artillery Museum, which opened in 1820. Grade II listed in 1973, the Rotunda was open to the public up until its closure, the artefacts on display relocated to Woolwich Firepower Museum, which closed permanently in 2016.

The Rotunda, now vacant, has been identified as of exceptional historical and architectural significance; however, the building is currently in a poor state of repair.

To the west of the Royal Artillery Barracks parade ground was Greenhill Barracks and regimental school. Post-Crimean emphasis on the importance of educating military personnel created a need to enlarge the school and provide education for non-commissioned officers, many of whom were illiterate, as well as educating children of military personnel.

By 1866, the school had taken the name Green Hill School, with a daily attendance of around 1,000 students. Before military use ended, the school buildings were considered for use as a museum after the future of the Rotunda was in question during the late 1960s.

Listed in 1973, the former Green Hill School buildings were unused until 1987–90 when converted by Parkview Estates into private residences, known as Greenhill Courts. At the front of the buildings, the 32-inch mortar, dating to 1854, is the largest ever constructed, and although never fired in war, could propel a shell around a mile and a half.

To the north of Greenhill Courts is the site of Red Barracks off Frances Street, commissioned as an infirmary for the Royal Marines, then, after the closure of the Royal Dockyard, the building passed to the British Army. The building, renamed Red Barracks due to its red-coloured bricks, housed personnel of the Army Ordnance Corps.

After the corps relocated to barracks at Portsmouth, the building became an army college and later home to the Inspectorate of Armaments and then the Royal Artillery record office. Decommissioned in 1967, although listed, the building was demolished, and the site was redeveloped for housing; only the Frances Street entrance and boundary wall survive.

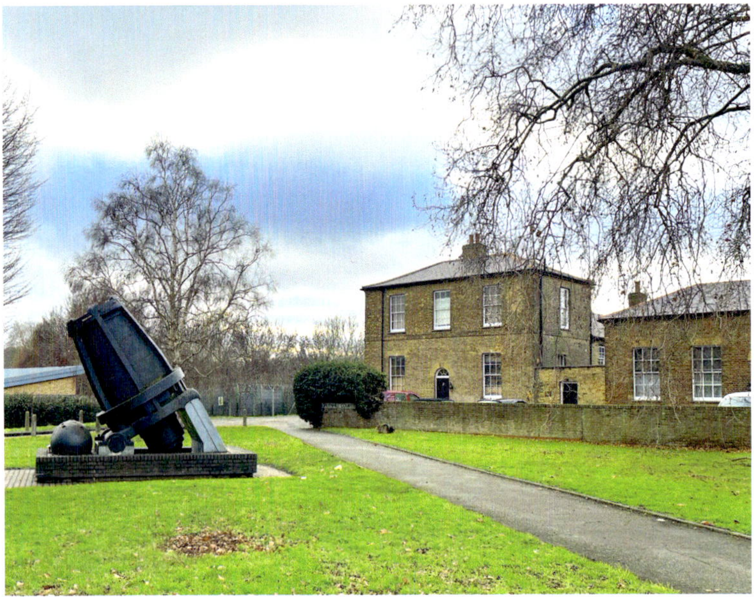

32-inch mortar in front of the former Greenhill School buildings.

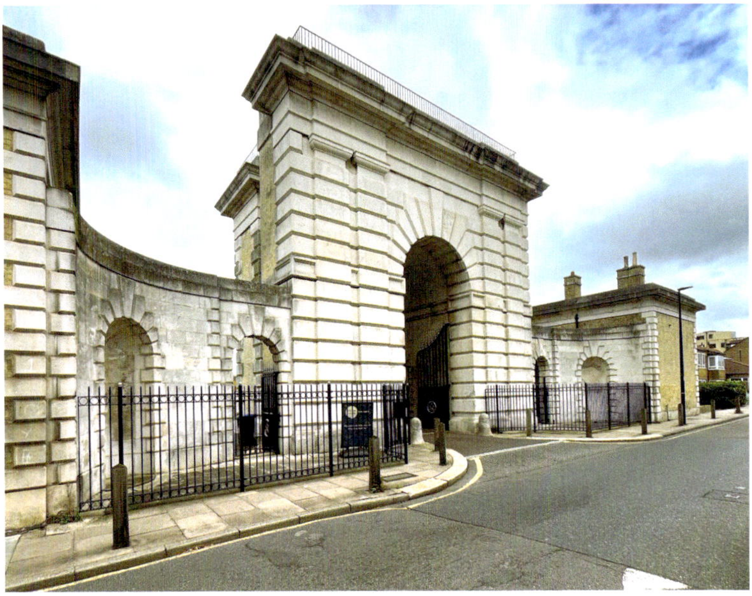

Original entrance to Red Barracks, Frances Street.

At the foot of Frances Street is the original main gate entrance to Woolwich Royal Dockyard, which is now a large residential estate. The most notable building to survive is the Grade II listed dockyard offices erected in 1783–84, now the refurbished Clockhouse Community Centre.

Leading off from the gates is a late eighteenth-century guard house, police station and Master Warder's lodgings, and apprentice school opposite, converted into accommodation.

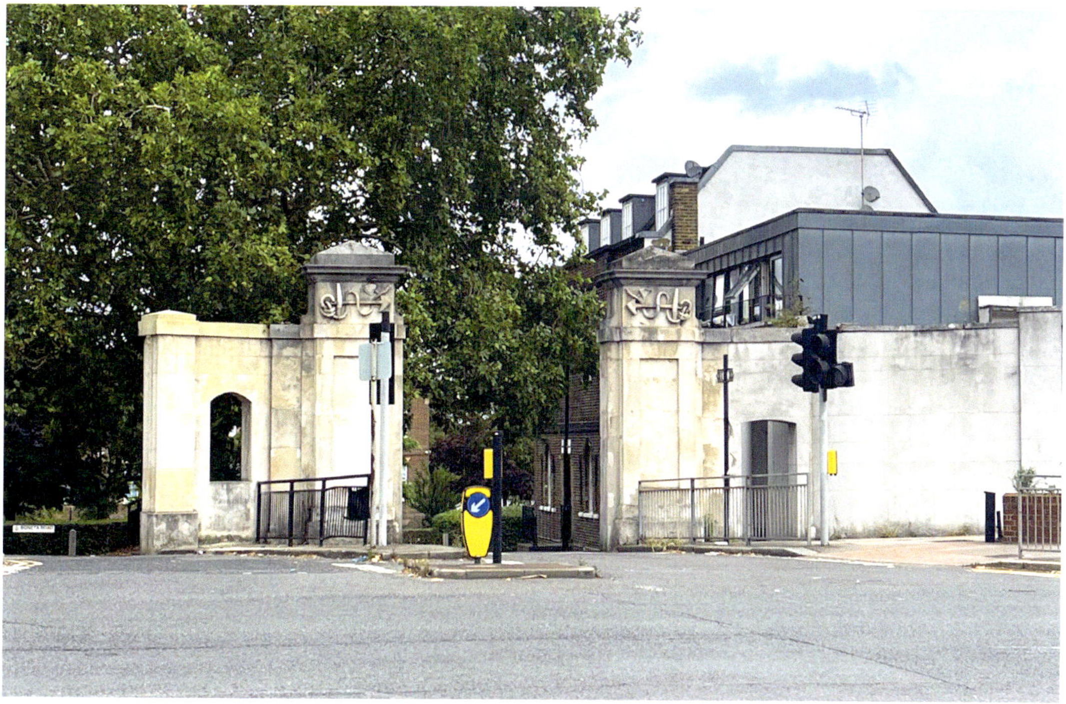

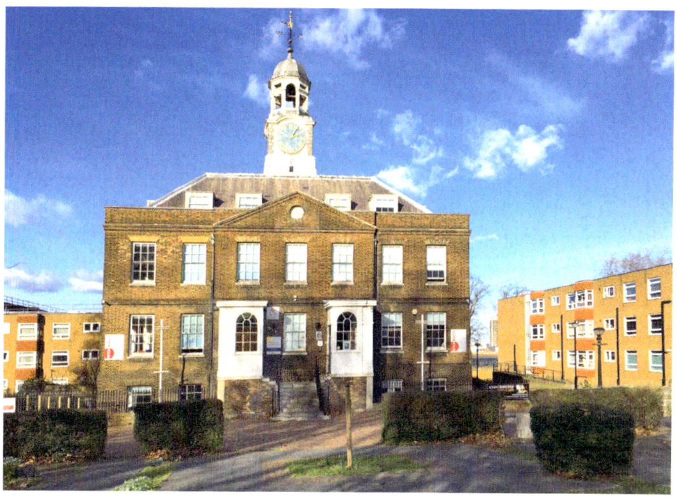

*Above*: Entrance gate to former Woolwich Royal Dockyard site.

*Right*: The Clock House, former dockyard offices, the earliest surviving Woolwich Dockyard building.

Other surviving industrial buildings include parts of the steam factory and its chimney, as well as sections of the dockyard perimeter wall.

Two shipbuilding slips survive, located between residential apartment blocks, and two drydock basins are awaiting redevelopment. After the dockyard's closure, several buildings were dismantled and re-erected at other sites, including the mid-nineteenth-century church rebuilt in Eltham.

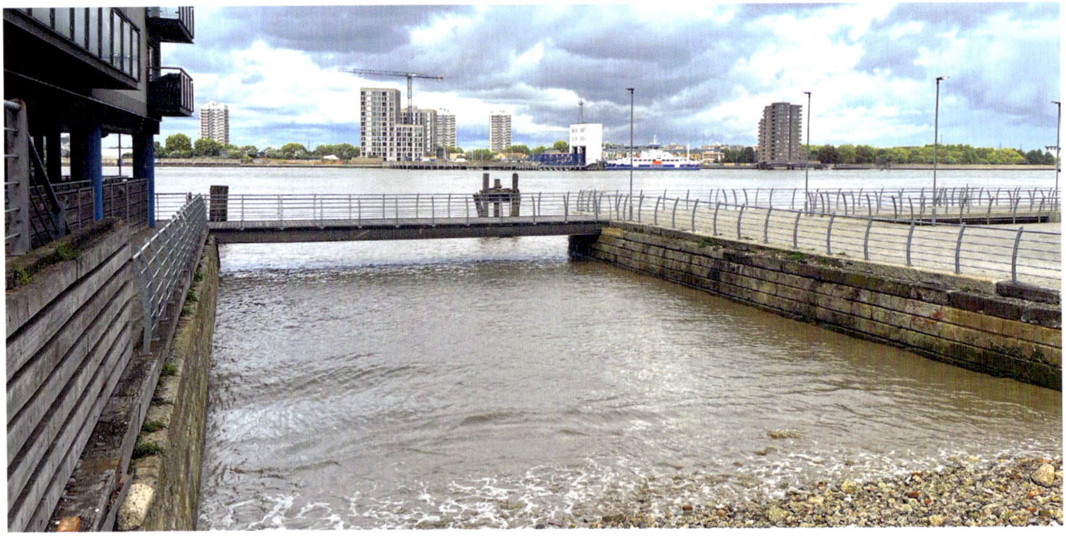

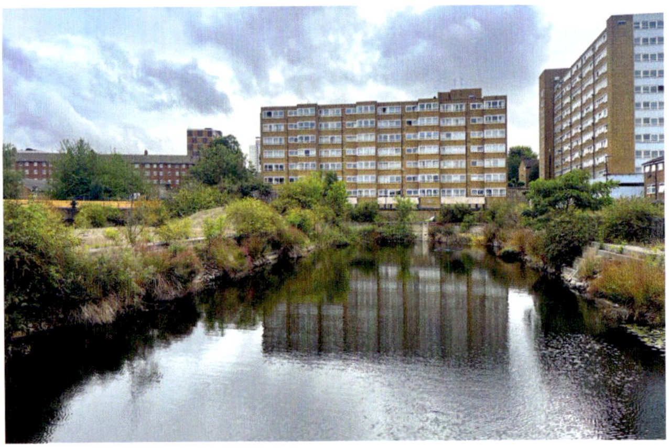

*Above*: The former Woolwich Royal Dockyard slipway opens to the Thames.

*Left*: Drydock basins filled with water and in use for fishing.

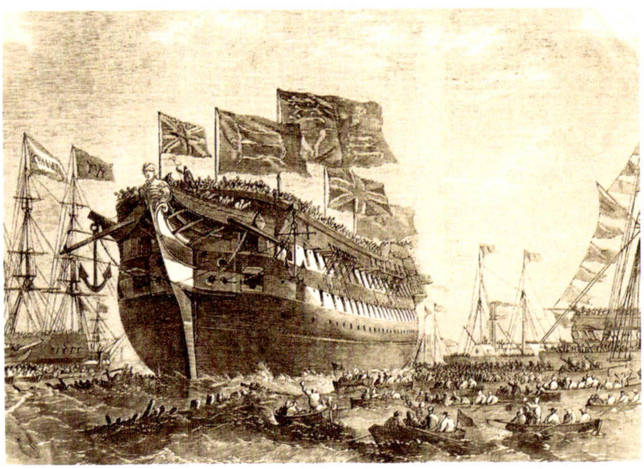

Woolwich-built HMS *Anson, c.* 1860, one of the last wooden-screw warships launched at Woolwich.

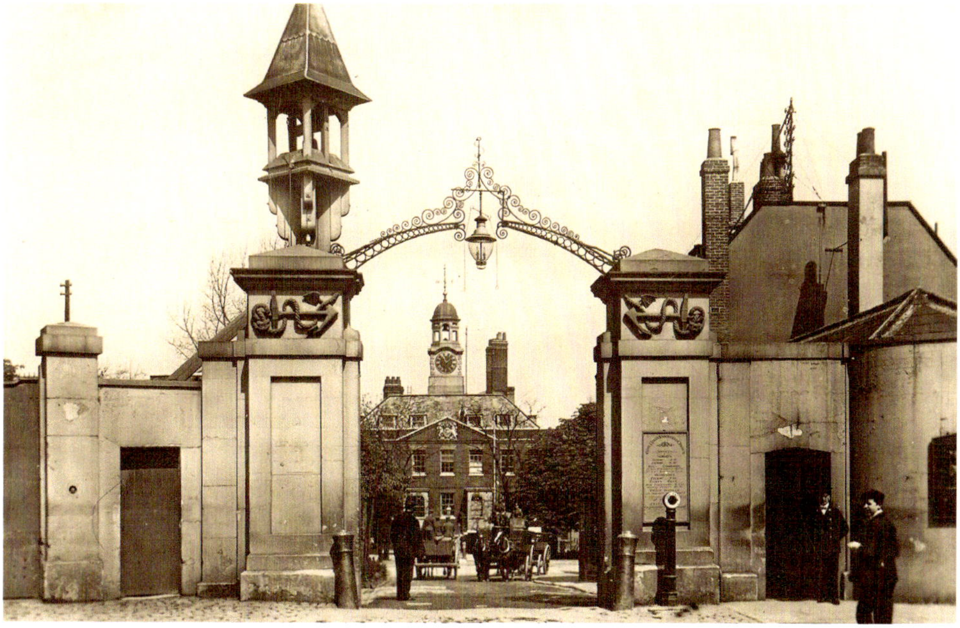

Woolwich Royal Dockyard main gate and bell tower, Woolwich Church Street, early 1900s.

To the east of the dockyard was the Royal Arsenal and although going through complete redevelopment, many of the site's historic buildings were retained, renovated, and refurbished for residential, leisure and commercial use.

The modernised mixed-use eighteenth- and nineteenth-century buildings include the Royal Brass Foundry, Royal Laboratory, Gun Foundry, Royal Military Academy, Storekeeper's House, Main Guard House, Royal Carriage Works, Grand Store Complex, Dial Square Workshop façade, Master Founder's House and various ancillary workshops and ordnance buildings.

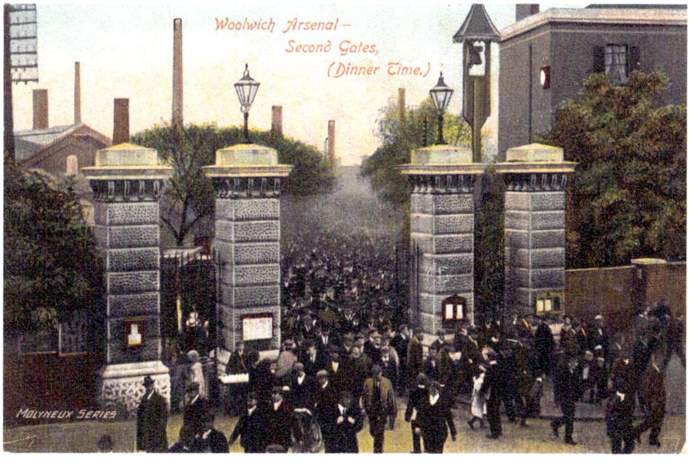


Woolwich Royal Arsenal second gate east of the Plumstead Road boundary wall, early 1900s.

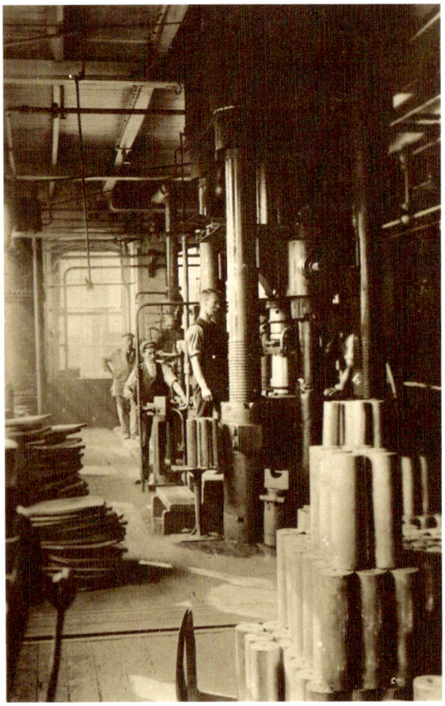

*Left*: Cartridge Factory No.1, producing quick-firing cartridges for artillery shells, early 1900s.

*Below*: Former Dial Square Workshop where workers founded Dial Square FC, later known as Arsenal FC.

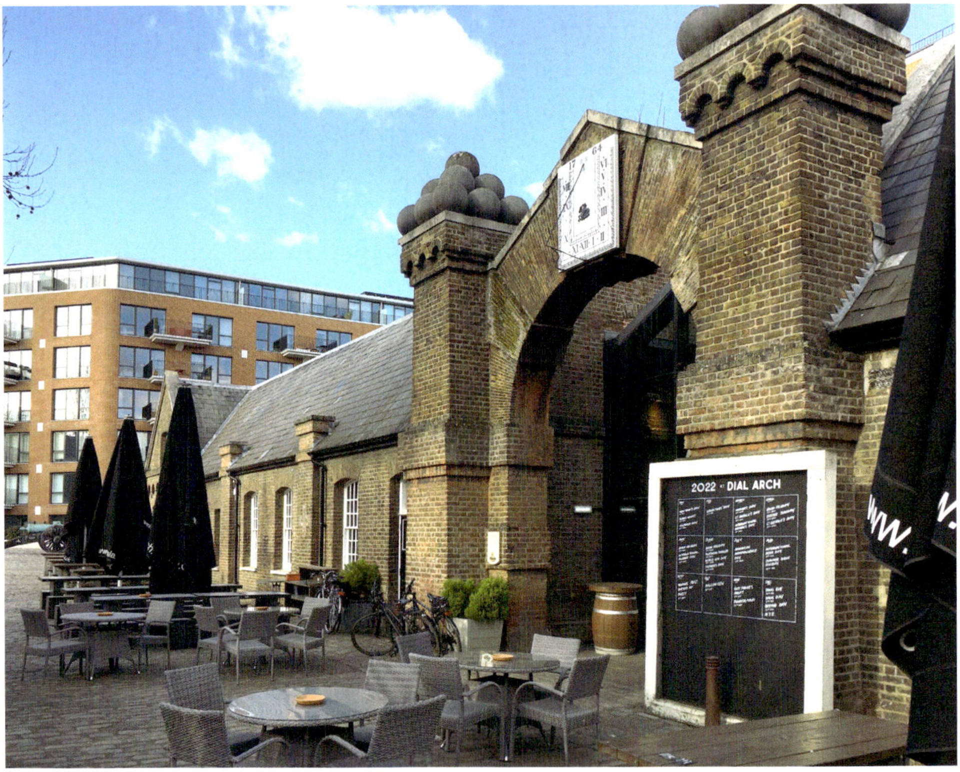

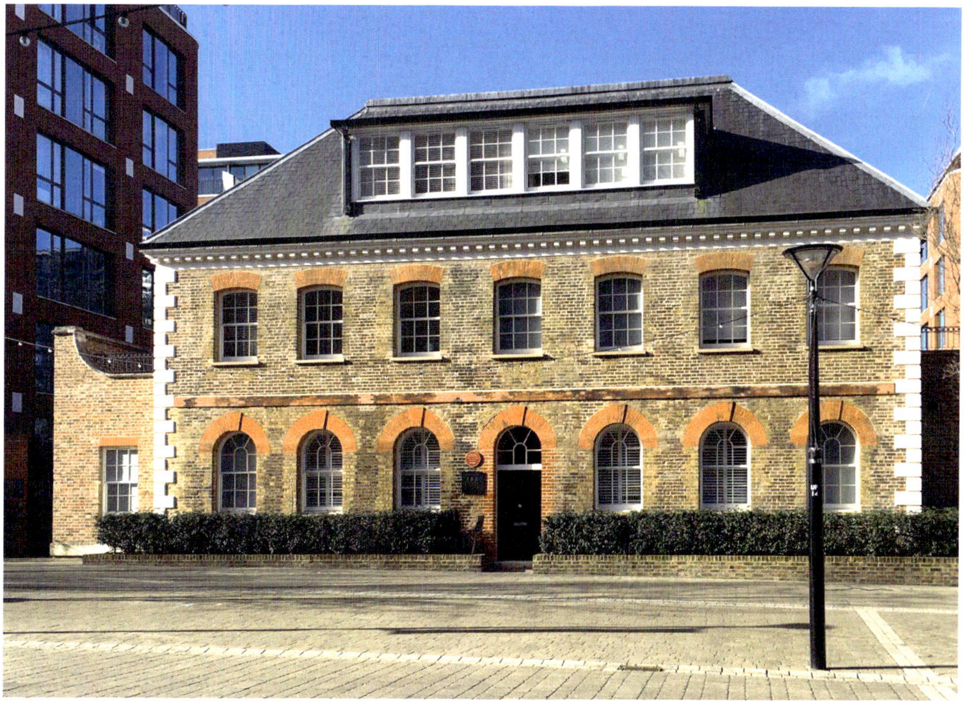

Laboratory East Pavilion, the oldest part of the Arsenal (late 1600s). One of a pair, where gunpowder was manufactured.

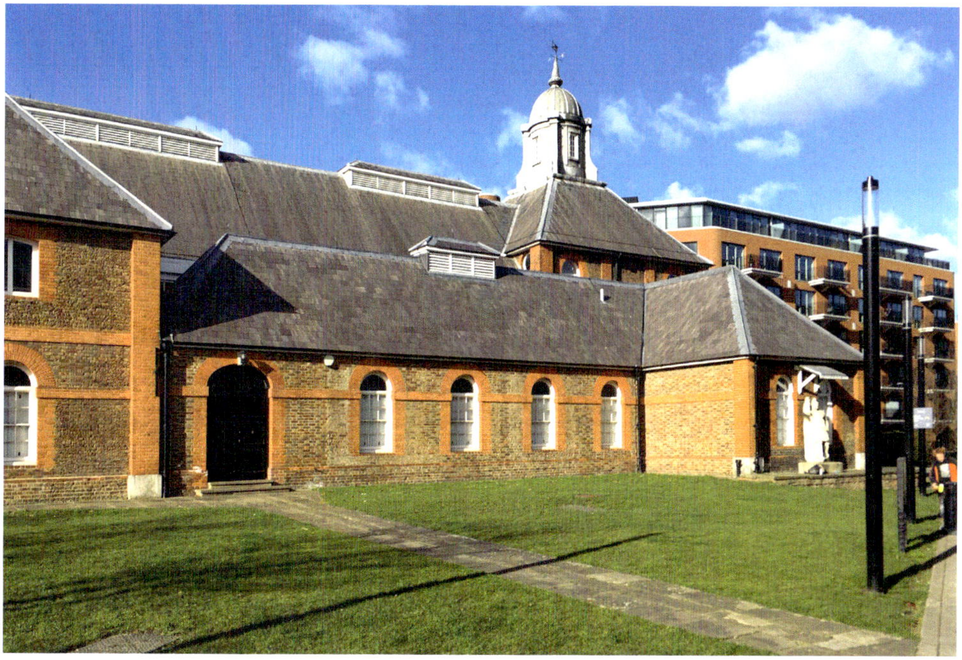

Former brass foundry, which housed furnaces and pouring pits for moulding guns, *c.* 1717.

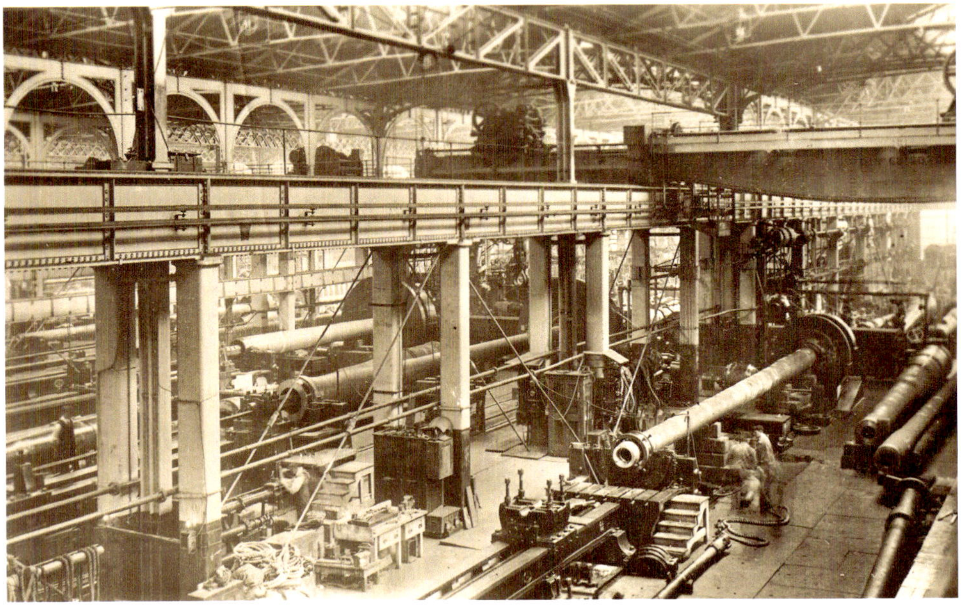

Boring mill for boring out, turning, and finishing barrels of large guns, *c.* 1900.

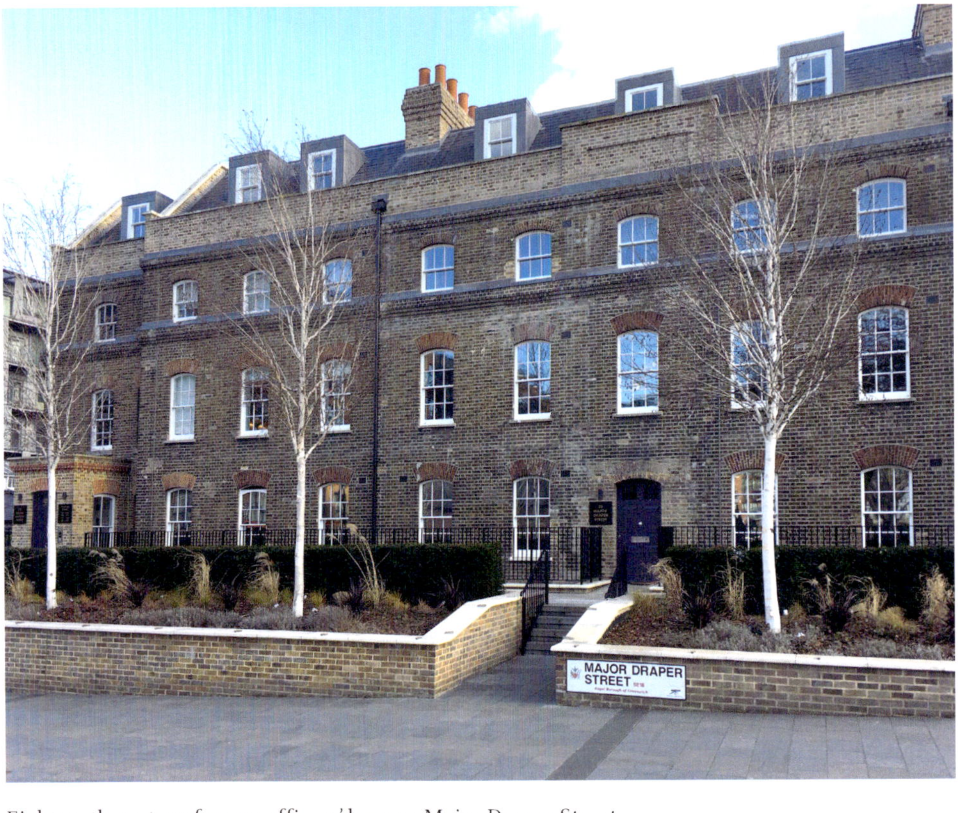


Eighteenth-century former officers' houses, Major Draper Street.

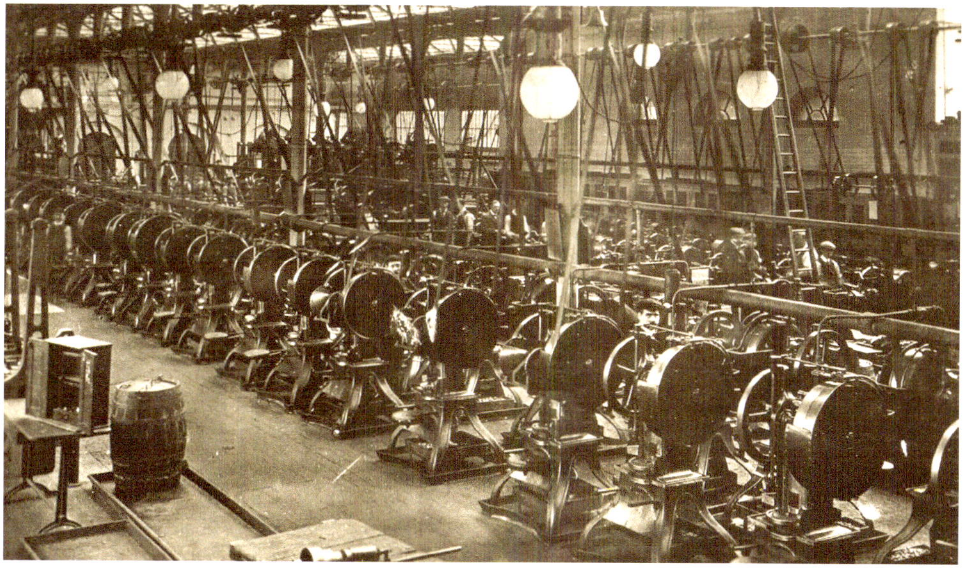

Bullet factory, early 1900s. Small arms bullets totalled over 1 billion 700 million during the Second World War.

When the main road from Woolwich to Greenwich was realigned, passing through the south of the Royal Arsenal in the 1980s, a new main gate and perimeter walls were erected, leaving the 1828-built Grade II listed Royal Arsenal Gatehouse, also known as Beresford Gatehouse after Master General of Ordnance William Beresford, outside the Arsenal site. Facing onto Beresford Square, the gatehouse was completely restored in the 1990s, with the square redeveloped in 2025.

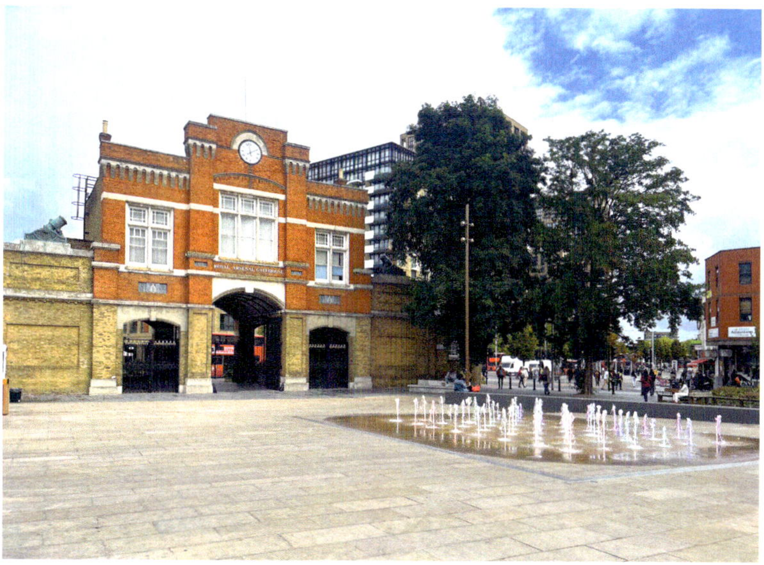

Woolwich Royal Arsenal main gate after refurbishment of Beresford Square, 2025.

# 6. Memorials and Statues

## Battle of Deptford Bridge

To the east of Blackheath, there is a contemporary installation to commemorate the Cornish archers, in the form of a circular sundial bench, located at Parkside, a contemporary development.

Decorated in a mosaic pattern representing a Celtic shield, a long steel arrow projecting from its centre acts as the sundial's gnomon. The long-gone Deptford Bridge once spanned the Ravensbourne River, close to the crossroads at the foot of Blackheath Road. Designed by Gary Drostle, the sundial was unveiled in 2017 by housing association, Family Mosaic, part of Peabody Trust.

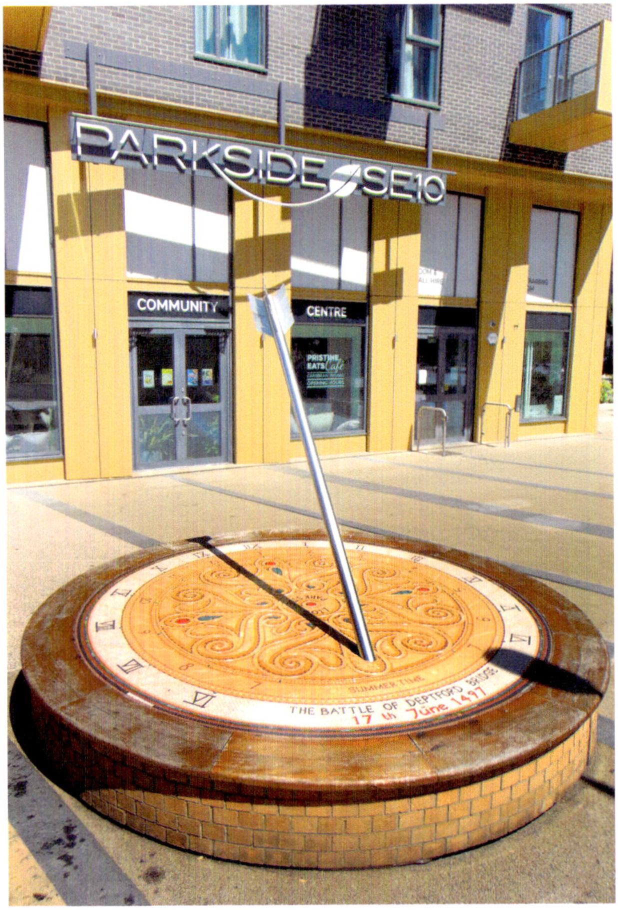


Battle of Deptford Bridge sundial, Parkside, Lewisham Road.

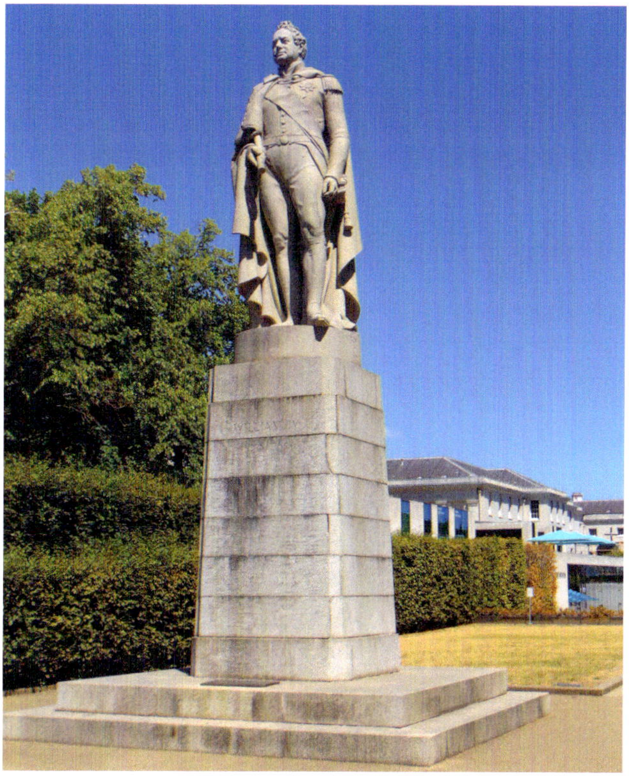

William IV, King William Walk.

## King William IV

Known as the 'Sailor King', a nickname William acquired after serving in the Royal Navy from the age of thirteen, the statue was relocated to Greenwich after road alterations at King William Street and Canon Street, London, in 1845. Dressed in the uniform of Lord High Admiral, the sculpture by Samuel Nixon was the first statue in London made of granite. The popular King William made many visits to Greenwich, accompanied by Queen Adelaide, formally and informally, to mark anniversaries of naval actions at sea, often meeting Greenwich Hospital pensioners who were veterans of those historic engagements.

## Devonport House Memorials

In the grounds of Grade II listed Devonport House, prior home for nurses working at the former Seaman's Hospital opposite, there are several memorials in remembrance of men and women associated with the naval hospital. The grounds had once been the cemetery for Greenwich Hospital pensioners and naval personnel, the remains of around 3,000 reinterred at a new site in 1875, East Greenwich Pleasaunce, to make way for the cut-and-cover built railway tunnel.

One small building is Devonport Mausoleum, the last resting place of various renowned naval figures. The most famous of those are Admiral Thomas Hardy, captain of HMS *Victory* at the Battle of Trafalgar, and Admiral Lord Hood, a noted admiral who commanded a British fleet to victory during America's War of Independence.

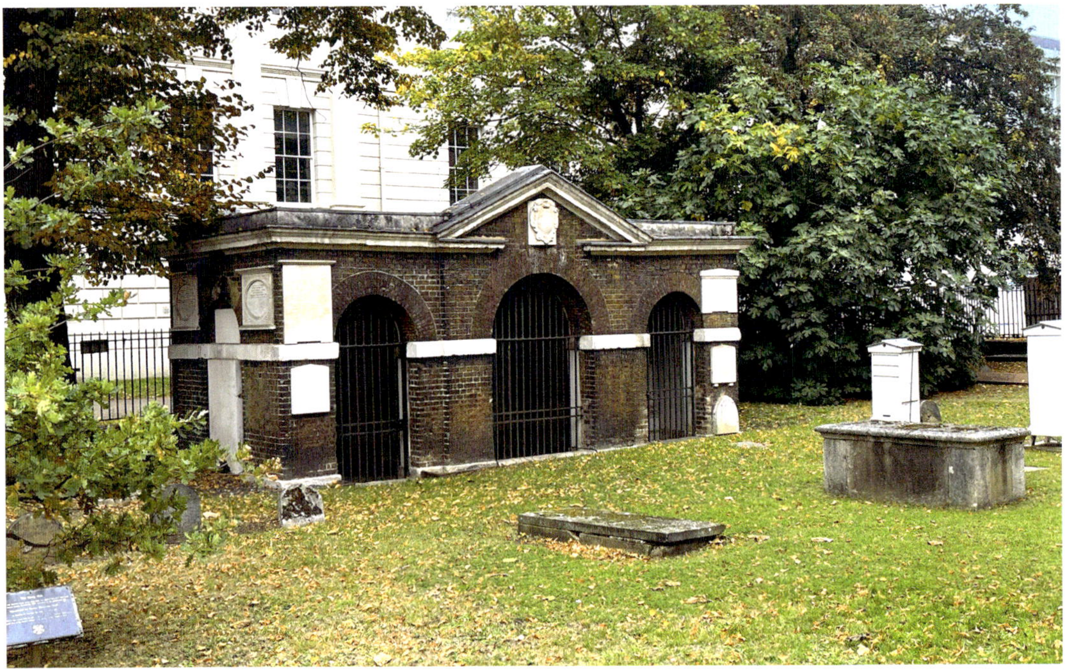

*Above*: Mausoleum, Devonport House.

*Below left*: Tom Allen memorial, Devonport House.

*Below right*: Memorial to the officers and men of the Royal Navy and Marines, Devonport House.

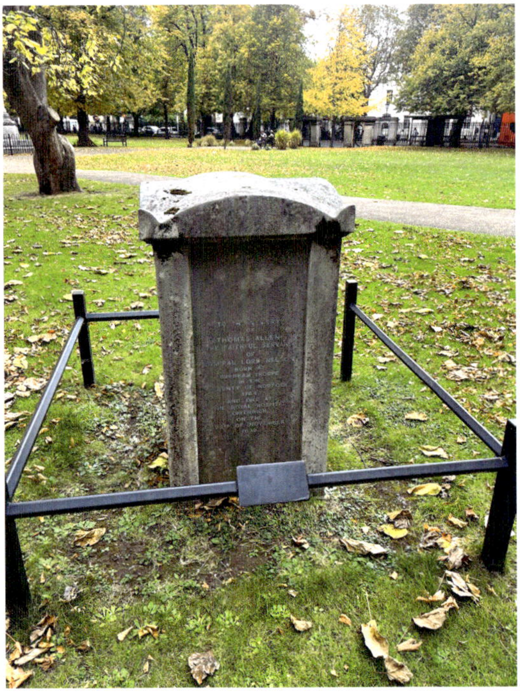

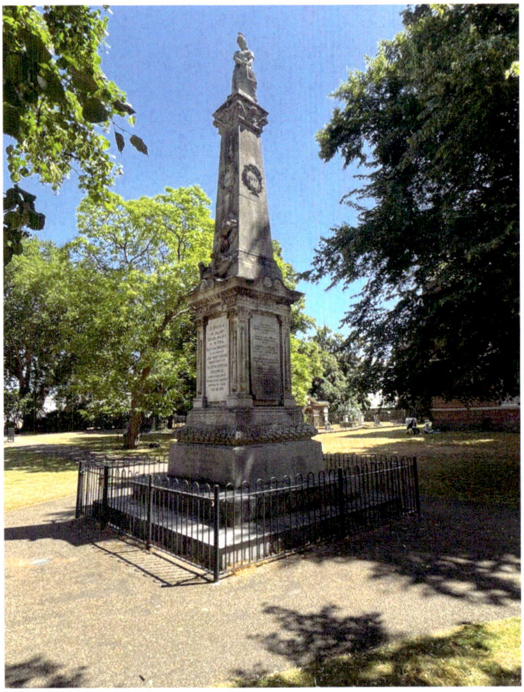

Close to the mausoleum is a stone memorial dedicated to Admiral Nelson's servant Tom Allen. Although not a naval seaman, he was admitted to Greenwich Hospital while Hardy was governor.

Other memorials are dedicated to the officers and men of the Royal Navy and Marines, Royal Navy officer and Controller of the Navy Sir Thomas Thompson, and John Simpson Esquire, Captain in Her Majesty's Fleet and Senior Captain of Greenwich Hospital.

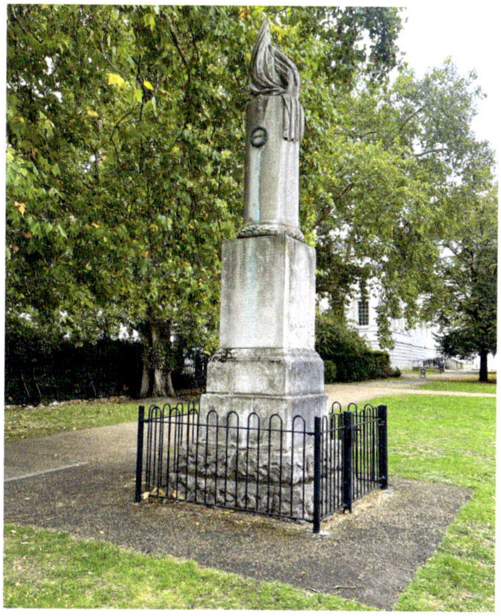

*Right*: Sir Thomas Thompson memorial, Devonport House.

*Below*: John Simpson Esquire memorial, Devonport House.

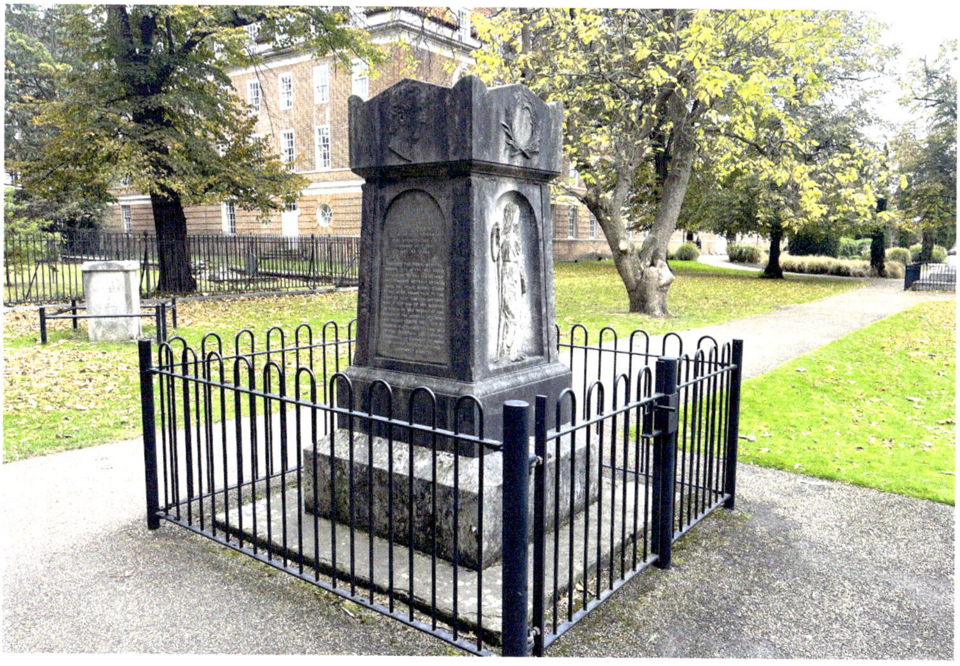

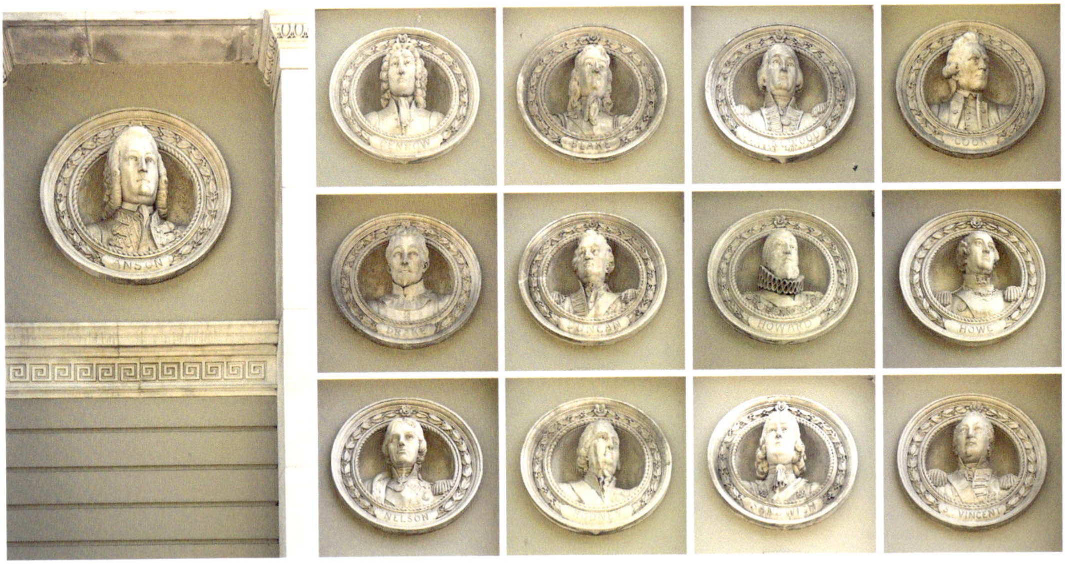


Medallion busts, Pepys Building, Discover Greenwich Visitor Centre.

## Pepys Building Medallion Busts

To the rear of the former Seaman's Hospital, the building named after Samuel Pepys is adorned on the north frontage with busts depicting famous maritime figures who played significant roles in British naval history.

The bust reliefs include Admiral George Anson; Admiral John Benbow; Admiral Thomas Blake; Admiral Cuthbert Collingwood; Captain James Cook; Sir Francis Drake; Admiral Adam Duncan; Admiral Thomas Howard; Admiral Richard Howe; Horatio Lord Nelson; Admiral George Bridges Rodney; Edward Montagu, 1st Earl of Sandwich and John Jervis, 1st Earl of St Vincent. The building, once in use as a squash and racket court for naval trainees and later an engineering laboratory, is now the Discover Greenwich Visitor Centre.

## Sir Walter Raleigh

The bronze statue of Sir Walter Raleigh was moved to Greenwich in 2001 from Old Palace Yard, Whitehall, close to where he was beheaded, and erected on the green at the entrance of the Discover Greenwich Visitor Centre.

Sculptured by William McMillan, the statue was first erected in 1959 to commemorate the 350th anniversary of the foundation of the Commonwealth of Virginia, Raleigh tasked by Elizabeth I to sail on an exploratory mission to the New World and establish a settlement, which Raleigh named Virginia after Elizabeth I, 'the Virgin Queen'. It has been speculated that close to the statue's current location is where Raleigh laid down his cloak over a muddy puddle for Elizabeth to walk across, saving the queen's feet from getting wet.

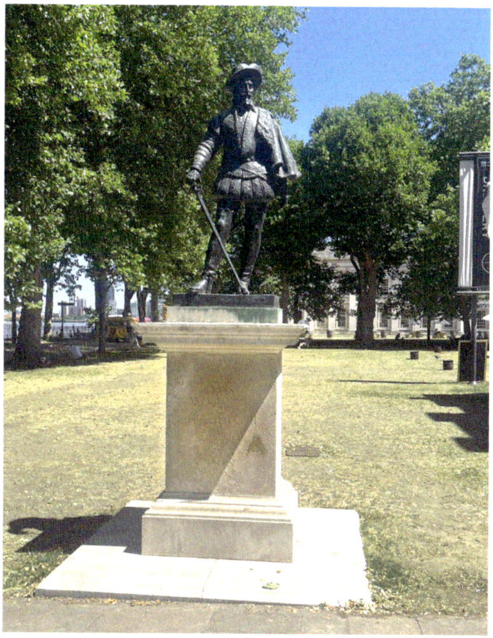

Sir Walter Raleigh, Cutty Sark Gardens.

## New Zealand Wars Monument

Constructed in 1872 from pink-grey Cornish granite, a tall obelisk north of Discover Greenwich Visitor Centre commemorates the officers and men of the Royal Navy who died in the 1863–64 New Zealand War.

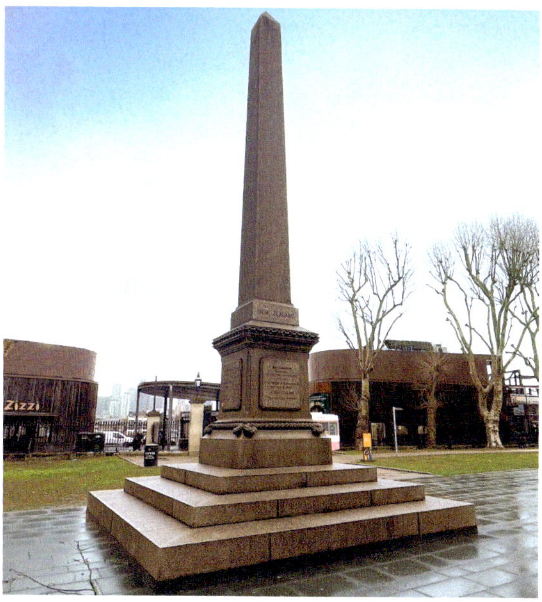


New Zealand Wars memorial, Cutty Sark Gardens.

The first hostilities in a series of wars began in the North Island between a federation of Māori tribes and the military forces of the colonial government over disputes surrounding European land settlements and colonisation.

## General James Wolfe

A gift from the people of Canada, the bronze statue of General James Wolfe stands high up on a stone plinth in Greenwich Park. Commander of British forces in a famous victory against the French at Quebec in 1759, Wolfe spent several years as a resident of Greenwich.

Made by Canadian sculptor Tait Mackenzie, the statue was unveiled on 5 June 1930 by the Marquis de Montcalm, a descendant of the French commander who also died during the battle. The tall stone plinth upon which Wolfe stands also shows signs of battle, having been scarred by shrapnel from an exploding bomb dropped during the Second World War.

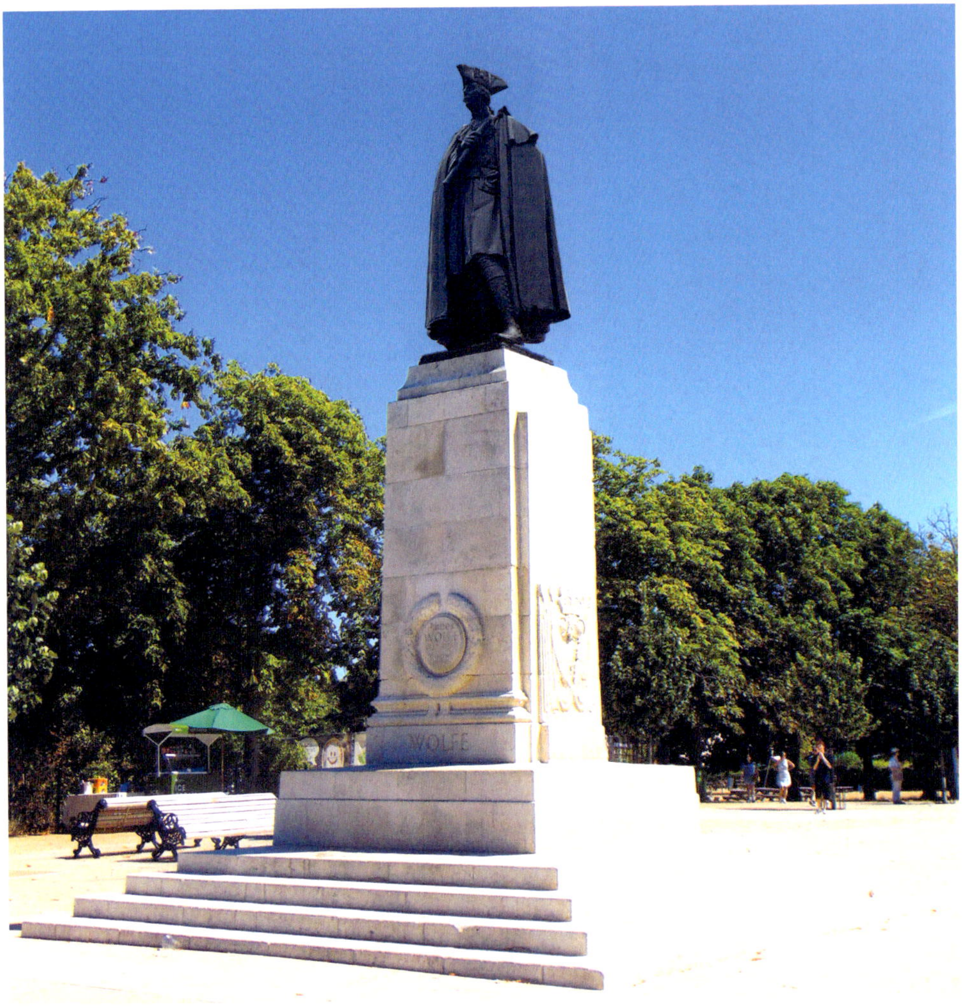


General James Wolfe, Greenwich Park.

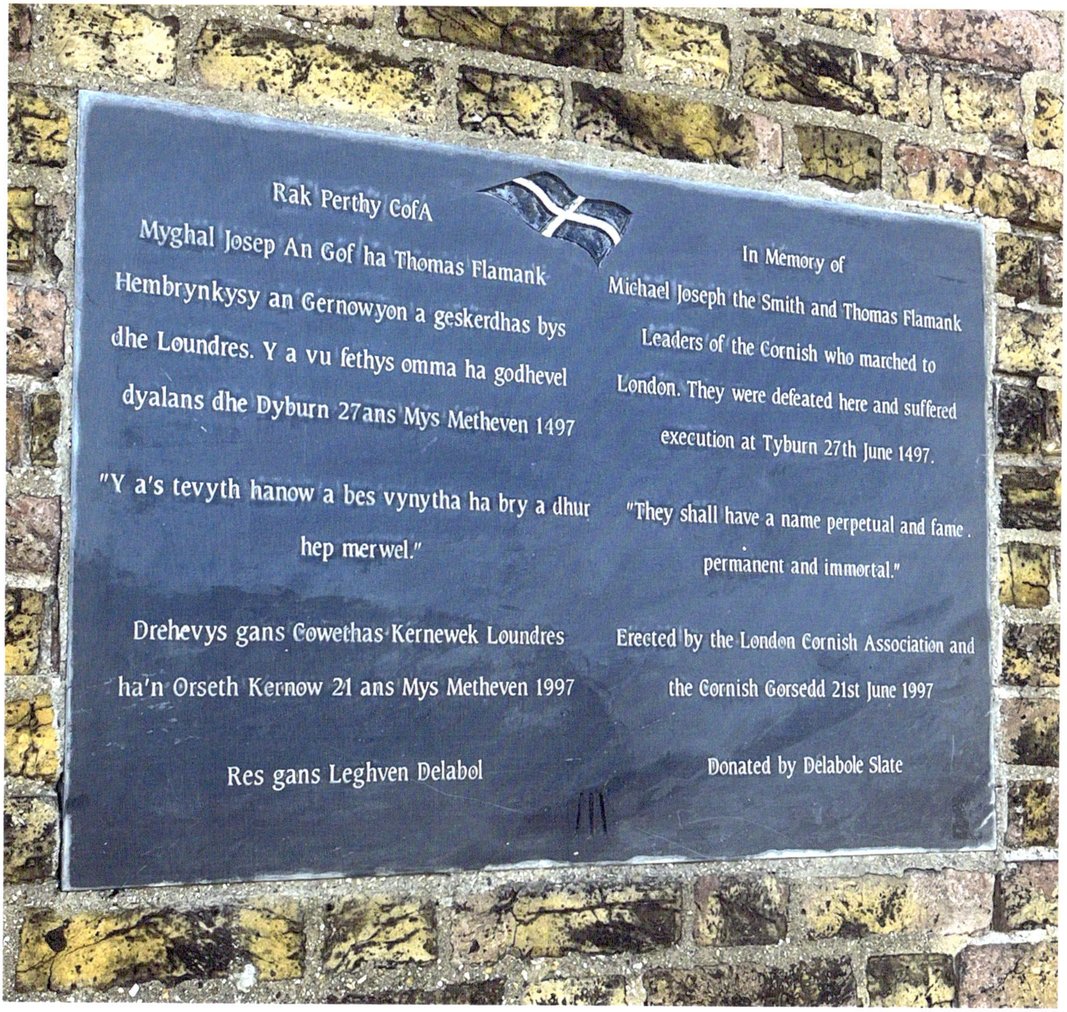


Cornish Rebellion plaque, Charlton Way, Blackheath.

## Cornish Rebellion

On the south side of the Greenwich Park boundary wall is a Cornish slate plaque commemorating the Battle of Blackheath, also referred to as the Battle of Deptford Bridge. Erected in 1997, the plaque is a memorial to the leaders of the rebellion, inscribed in both Cornish and English.

## Blackheath War Memorial

In remembrance of residents of the borough who lost their lives in both world wars, a memorial located at the south-east corner of Greenwich Park bears the Royal Borough of Greenwich coat of arms, along with the poignant Latin motto below: *Tempore Utimur* ('We Use Time'). The Grade II listed memorial, constructed in Portland stone, was unveiled on Armistice Day 1922 by Harry Bolton Sewell, father of Greenwich-born Lt Cecil Sewell VC.

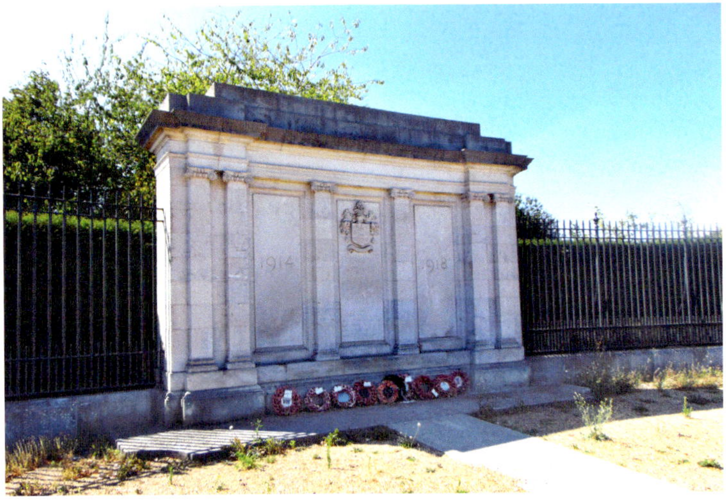


War memorial, Maze Hill, Blackheath.

## East Greenwich Gasworks Memorial

At Greenwich Peninsula, once a large industrial site heavily bombed during the Second World War, stands a memorial dedicated by the Bishop of Southwark in 1926 inscribed with the names of seventy-nine employees of the gasworks who lost their lives serving the country during the First World War. Unveiled by Dr Charles Carpenter, President of the South Metropolitan Gas Company, a guard of honour was provided by the 302nd Anti-Aircraft Battalion, Royal Engineers. Following the closure of the gasworks, the memorial was relocated a short distance to the Millennium Complex development, Central Park, and re-dedicated in 1999.

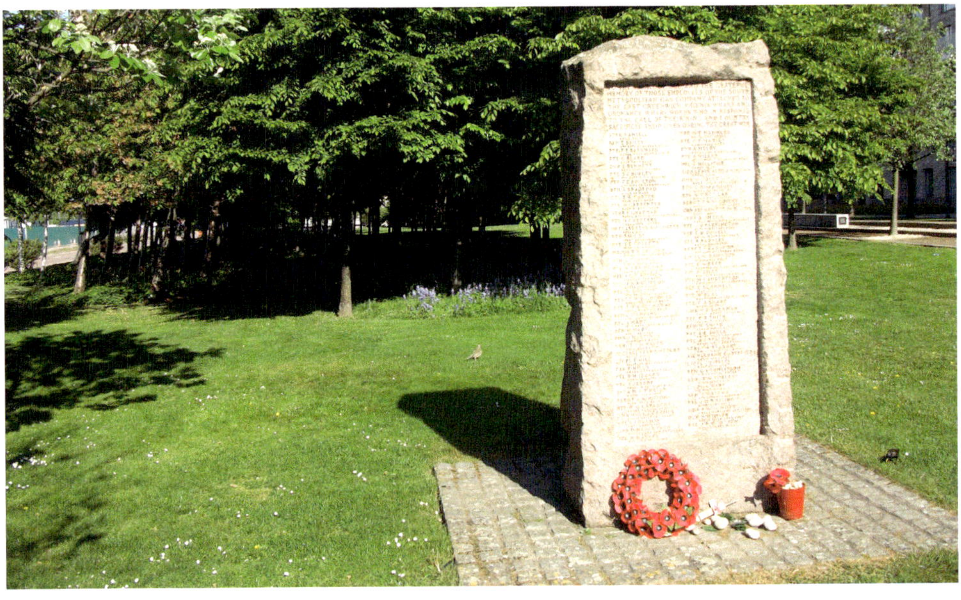

East Greenwich gasworks memorial, John Harrison Way.

## Woolwich Board of Ordnance Memorial

Within the Royal Arsenal armaments site, attached to the corner of Building 37, is a memorial plaque dedicated to the sixty-five men of the Army Ordnance Department who gave their lives during the First World War. Originally, there were two identical memorials dedicated to the Army Ordnance Department: one erected in the Royal Arsenal and the other in the adjacent dockyard.

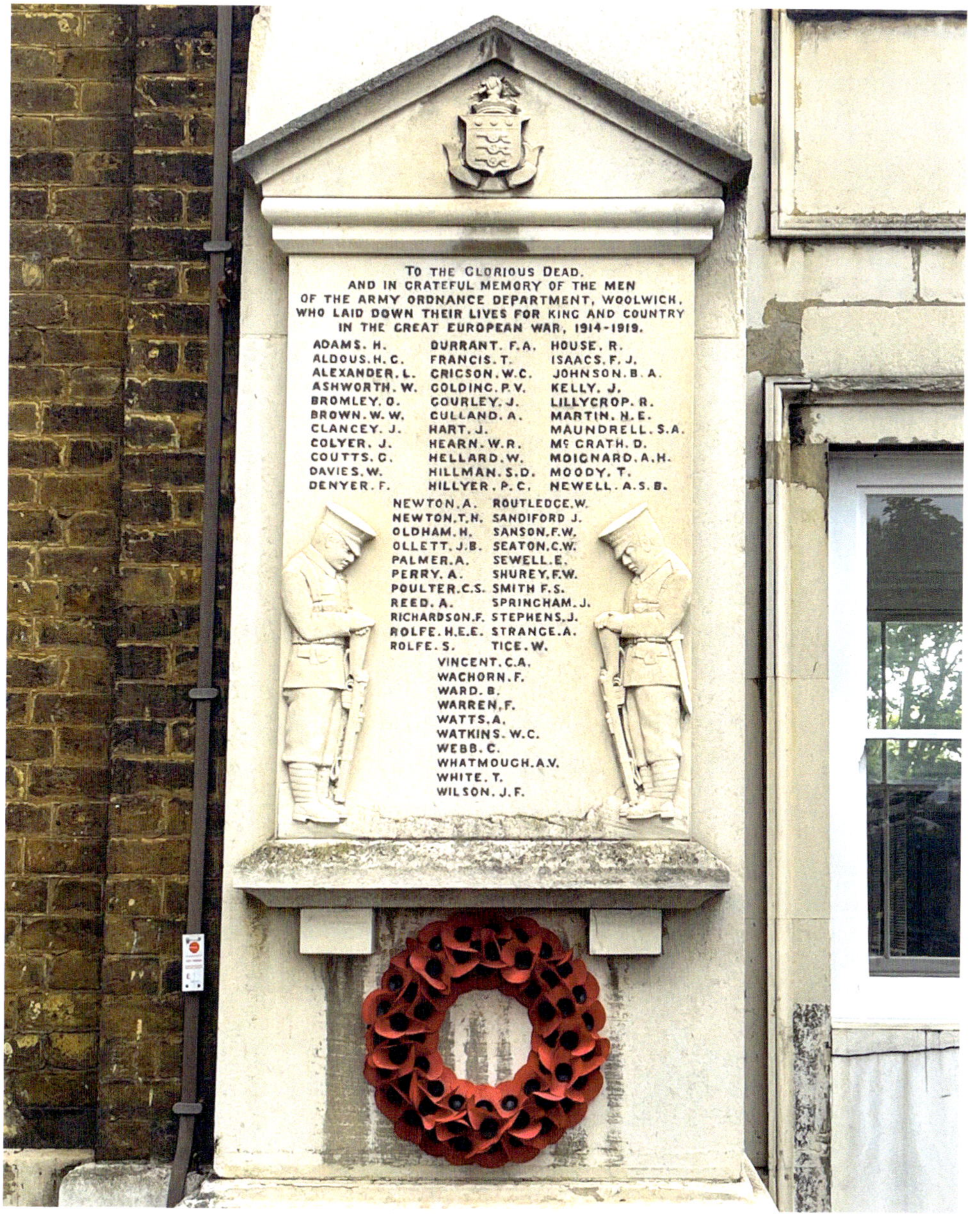


Woolwich Board of Ordnance Memorial, Woolwich Royal Arsenal.

# Bibliography


Aslet, Clive, *The Story of Greenwich* (Fourth Estate Limited, 1999)

Besant, Sir Walter, *Early London, Prehistoric, Roman, Saxon and Norman* (Adam and Charles Black, 1908)

Ed, Hibbert, Christopher and Weinreb, Ben, *The London Encyclopaedia* (Book Club Associates1983)

Jerrold, Walter, *Highways and Byways in Kent* (Macmillan and Co., 1924)

*Kelly's Directory of Kent* (London, Kelly & Co., 1882)

Rhind, Neil and Watson, Julian, *Greenwich Revealed* (Blackheath Society)

Vincent, William Thomas, *Warlike Woolwich a History Guide* (A.W. and J. P. Jackson, 1885)

## Websites

Air-Britain

British-History Online

Dover-Kent Archives

Graces Guide

Greenwich Industrial History Society

Historic-UK

Kidbrooke Village London

National Archives

Ideal-Homes History of Southeast

Ideal-Homes Greenwich

Old Maps Online

Old Royal Naval College

Royal Arsenal History

Royal Museums Greenwich

Staged Skirmish RMG

University College London

Victorian Web

Vision of Britain

Wellcome Collection

# Acknowledgements

The author would like to thank the following for their assistance in research for this publication: Dr John Black, Ian Bull, Dean Edwards, Mike Goodger, Karen Link, Chris Mansfield, Geoff Nutkins, Steven Peterson, Katarzyna Podkowik, Jayne Shakeshaft, officers and personnel of Woolwich Royal Artillery Barracks, the author's family members and postcard fair retailers who have assisted in locating various images and photographs. If, for any reason, I have not accredited people or organisations as necessary, I apologise for any oversight, and will make the necessary correction at the first opportunity.

## Photographs

Many thanks to the following for use of images: A. Phinbow (p. 61), Dover Publications (p. 25), Geoff Nutkins and Mike Goodger Shoreham Aircraft Museum (p. 49), Dr John Black (p. 59), Greenwich Heritage Centre (p. 29), Wellcome Collection (p. 23, 33, 34, 35, 36, 37, 38, 39, 40, 41, 42, 43, 44, 45, 58) and Woolwich Royal Artillery Barracks (p. 53).

# About the Author

Born in Greenwich, London, David Ramzan has always had a keen interest in the history of his hometown and studied local history as an undergraduate at the University of Oxford. A self-employed graphic designer, illustrator, and artist, he also worked in special educational needs and has written several historical publications and articles for magazines and periodicals on subjects including local history, maritime and football history, piracy, smuggling, and Victorian crime.

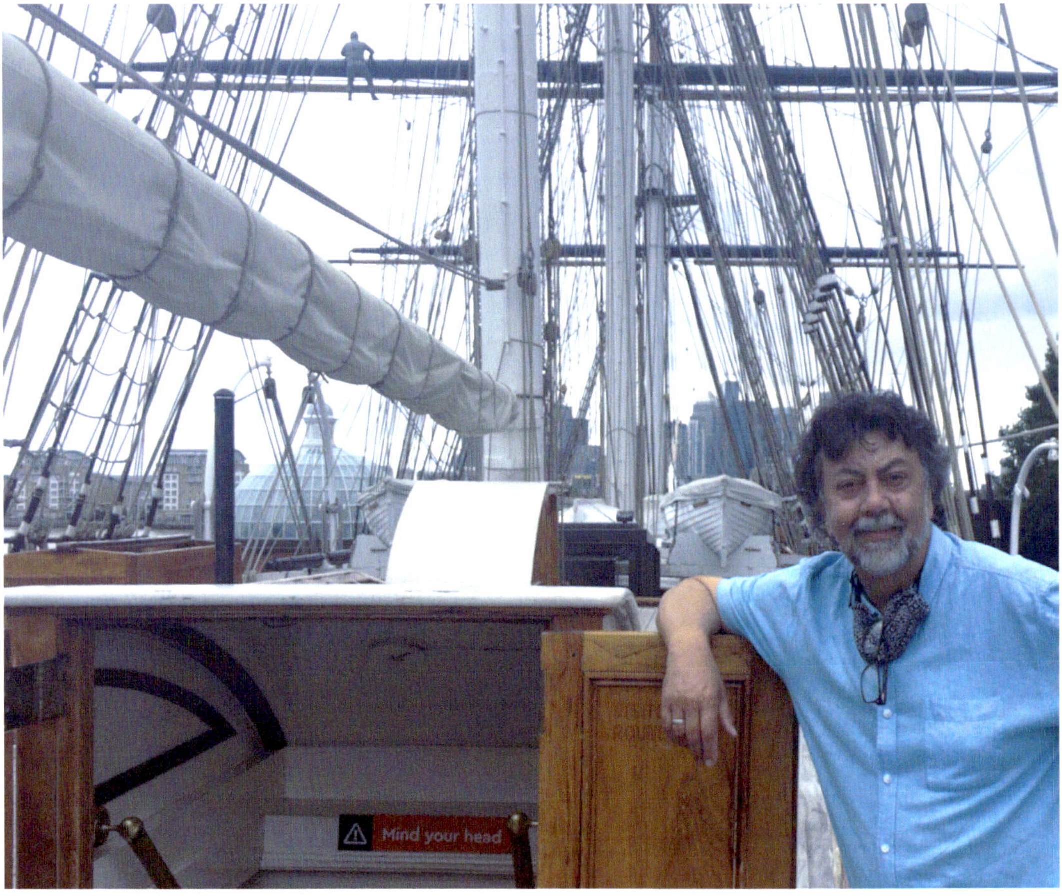


Author, David C. Ramzan.